Home Fiesta

D1830782

Home Fiesta

Chandrama Majumdar

GenNext Publication

© **Author**

All rights reserved. No part of this book may be reproduced, stored, adapted, or transmitted in any form or by any means, electronic, mechanical, photocopying, micro-filming recording or otherwise, or translated in any language, without the prior written permission of the copyright owner and the publisher. The book is sold subject to the condition that it shall not, by way of trade or otherwise, be lent, resold, hired out, or otherwise circulated without the prior publisher's written consent in any form of binding or cover other than that in which it is published.

The views and opinions expressed in this book are author(s) own and the facts reported by them have been verified to the extent possible, and the publishers are not in any way liable for the same.

ISBN : 978-93-5128-052-1

Price : ₹ 299

First Published 2015

Published by

GenNext Publications
23, Main Ansari Road,
Dariyaganj, New Delhi-110002
Ph. : 23282060, 23261060
E-mail: gennext@hotmail.com

Laser Typesetting : Shubham Printers, Delhi
Printed at : G. Print Process, Delhi

Cataloging in Publication Data—DK
Courtesy: D.K. Agencies (P) Ltd. <docinfo@dkagencies.com>

Majumdar, Chandrama.
Home fiesta / Chandrama Majumdar.
p. cm.
ISBN 9789351280521

1. Housekeeping—Handbooks, manuals, etc. 2. Home economics—Handbooks, manuals, etc. 3. Cooking, Indic. 4. Cookbooks. I. Title.

DDC 648 23

Contents

Acknowledgements

The following people have influenced me deeply for what I am today.

My heartfelt gratitude and acknowledgement for -

1. My Grandmother Late Renuka Devi.
2. My Baropishi and Pisho (Mr. Aniruddha Chakladar & Mrs. Dipali Chakladar, Slough, United Kingdom)
3. My childhood best friend's parents (Mr. Pradyut Kumar Bose & Mrs. Mitra Bose, Kolkata).
4. My Barokaku (Capt. Pradip Kumar Nath, retired Executive Director, IISCO)
5. My childhood friend's mother Late GautumiRahut.

Also this book would not have been possible without the love, blessings and unconditional support from my loved ones in this journey of mine.

1. My Parents (Mr. Dilip Kumar Nath& Mrs. Manjushree Nath).
2. All my Pishis. (Mrs Anita Das, Kolkata, Mrs. Sikha Sarkar, Fortworth, U.S.A. & Mrs. Santa Mukerjee, Kolkata)
3. Dr. Rashmi Choudhri (Principal, Podar School (CIE), Nerul)
4. Dr. Seema Singh (Ex. Coordinator,Podar School)
5. All my staff and colleague of Podar International School with special mention for Smita Kodukula, Mrs Ritu Verma & Ms. Aditi Yagnik (for photographs)
6. My 2 sons Aniket & Anubhab Majumdar.

This Book is dedicated to my father on his 75th birthday (28th Sept)

Introduction

When a guest enters the threshold of a domestic household, the persona of the homemaker is reflected first and foremost. So it is wisely said that 'It is easier to become a model while tough to become a homemaker.'

Today's homemaker is no longer limited within the territory of the kitchen and the courtyard. Women are increasingly stepping out of their threshold to achieve economic independence and the benefits are double income in the family to enjoy whatever the materialistic world has to offer. The present day demands that you play many roles expecting you to be almost omnipresent!

With more and more families turning 'nuclear', the onus of managing homehearth and 'beyond' has fallen on the matriarch of the home. Her responsibilities involve buying grocery, paying utility bills, picking up children from school, attending to their study, engaging help for repair and the list goes on.

Here's a sampler :

At School

- Attending Parent Teacher Meetings;
- Going for counseling sessions
- Participating in school activities like exhibitions, school project, science fair, annual day, sports meet, etc.

Outside School

Taking them to hobby classes/tuitions

At home

Regular chores like cooking, cleaning and managing children.

Keeping track of purchase for daily, weekly and monthly needs.

Storing efficiently for ease and saving time.

Stacking and managing linens, white clothes, etc.

Managing children's tantrums.

Taking a sick child to the doctor.

Society

Social gatherings and festivals

Family functions

My observations in some of the kitchens and the other rooms from cities like Delhi, Mumbai and Kolkata have revealed dirty filthy kitchens and totally unkept rooms. Starting from the kitchen racks to the kettles, from ceilings to the containers, the fans to the fridge, everything is crying out '*help*'. An archeological survey inside the refrigerator will bring out several small packets of unused items which now have accumulated fungus. Several expired items will be sitting with pride on the shelf!

It was necessary for me to give you a brief synopsis of the reality before plunging in to the sacred business of giving advice. In the following chapters I have made an elaborate attempt at providing you with all the necessary guidance which when followed properly will help you "To stay easy even white being busy."

If one learns the tricks of efficient housekeeping and kitchen management from an expert housekeeper, one can free oneself more from the persistent demands of the day to enjoy hobbies and other pursuits. Such a home keeper is the true winner!

1
Great Tips Related to You and Your Cooking

I personally feel it is necessary to have a rational and scientific approach in any task, no matter how mundane it is. In general suggestions are implemented effectively when it is backed by scientific or logical reasoning. I have tried to put them wherever it was possible.

Coconut

How to Store

Coconut Scraping

Scrape the coconuts (try to buy fresh tender variety). Put it inside the zip lock bag. Place it on the table or kitchen countertop or on any other flat surface. Remember it should be clean. Then with the palm of your hand, press the zip lock bag from the bottom towards the mouth of the bag. Keep the mouth of the bag open. The content should be placed inside the bag in such a way so as to make it a thin layer like a sheet. The excess should be taken out with a clean spoon and stored in the same way in another bag. Then place this bag on any shelve of the freezer. Once set it should look like a sheet of ice. While making any preparation, take out the bag. Take out the required quantity needed (either for any individual dish or the total amount for several dishes). By taking out I mean, simply break the quantity you require and keep it in a bowl. After it thaws, you will get freshly made coconut scrapings.

Examples : Suppose you have plans to make idli with coconut chutney (requiring half cup of coconut scrapings) for breakfast, Malwani/Konkani style fish gravy (requiring one cup of coconut scrapings)/maybe Bengali prawn Malaikari where you would require generous amount of coconut milk. Now your task is to calculate the total amount of coconut scrapings you need and take it out, in this case, say approximately one and a half cup. Once thawed, use it immediately. If you do not want to make the second dish due to some inconvenience, never put it back to the freezer. Instead keep it inside a bowl and cover it. Place it in the freeze and use within 24 hours.

Note: Never make a thick sheet. It would be difficult to break it.

Onion

(i) The Science behind Onion Tears

1. Onion contains a substance known as propenesulfenic which is solely responsible for bringing tears in the eyes.
2. When an onion is cut, cells are ruptured, which release enzymes resulting in breaking down of sulfur compounds into oxides (propanethiol S-oxide), a volatile sulfur compound. This is attracted to water and wet places. As eyes are the closest thing to the cut onion that contains moisture, the vapour gets attracted to it and forms a mild acid, which irritates the eye and stimulates the tear glands. The chemicals in the onion are both volatile and water soluble.
3. This gas reacts with the water in the tears to form sulfuric acid. The sulfuric acid burns, stimulating one's eyes to release more tears to wash the irritant away.

(ii) Effective Ways to Prevent Onion Tears

1. **ALWAYS USE A sharp knife** and apply the proper technique of chopping onions. This ruptures fewer onion cells, thus lessening the amount of gas in the air.

2. **You can try cutting them near an open flame.** The flame is supposed to draw in air, thereby preventing the gas to come in contact with one's eyes.
3. **Chilling the onion for ½-1** hour before chopping them will minimize the amount of enzymes that are released while cutting of onions, thereby reducing the volatility of the sulfide.
4. Rubbing some **vinegar on to the cutting board before cutting** interrupts the chemical reaction.
5. Last but probably the most effective one is to wear **Swimming Goggles** during the whole cutting, slicing and chopping process to prevent those onion tears.

(iii) Proper Technique of Cutting an Onion

Though it might appear stupid to most of you, it's important to know which one is the root end because this end releases more of that gas responsible for tears. Therefore our focus should also lie in trying to keep it intact as long as possible.

First Step–Cut the onion in half right through the stem and the root.

Second Step–Cut off the stem end.

Third Step–Now, peel off the outer layers of skin very easily.

Fourth Step–Try making cuts in the onion without cutting all the way through the root end. That is, you have to ensure keeping the root end intact. The space between your cuts should depend upon your preferences for it.

In this way, the onion should hold together at the root end.

Last Step–Cut across the onions crosswise to get perfect diced onions.

Note : The size of the dice can be varied by making fewer cuts across the onion.

(iv) Ways of Getting Rid of the Odour

You can lightly wet your hands and then rub a little bit of soda / lemon all over your hands. Then rinse your hands well.

(v) Tips for Browning of Onions

1. Onions turn softer and pinkish when salt is added to it. To make it brown you have to fry it further.
2. Onions will also brown faster if it is fried with a pinch of sugar.

To reduce your cooking time, you can fry your entire onion requirement at one time and brown them. Then keep it separately for the different dishes.

Example : You need them for Chicken, Fish, Chana ki dal, Garnishing purpose, etc. Fry them (atleast one kg) together and use separately as required.

Brown Onion Paste–Heat a kadai. Put raw onion paste into it. Add some seasoning and sauté it for a while. It will take approx. 15 mins for the water to evaporate away. Now you can add a tablespoon of oil. Keep it on simmer, stirring occasionally till you have attained the pinkish brown colour. Now for storing, I normally keep it in several containers and keep all but one in the Freezer. The other one goes in the Fridge. Follow the same procedure for **fried sliced onions**. Whenever I need some for Non-veg/chole/Rajma, I get it instantly. When it finishes, I take one container from the Freezer and keep it in the fridge. It will get thawed naturally and you can use this onion paste for the next week. Likewise you can use the rest of the containers.

Ginger

(1) **Ginger Peel** – Take about half a kilo of ginger and soak it in water for an hour. This will loosen the dirt. Wash it clean

and peel the ginger with the help of a peeler or a kitchen knife. Store the ginger peel in the same manner like coconut. You can use them to make your ginger tea.

Note : You have to use a large proportion, because it is peel and not ginger.

(2) **Ginger Paste** – After peeling the ginger, cut the whole ginger into one inch pieces. You can also trim the corners and vents if you want to. Now make a smooth paste in a blender by adding enough water. Remember it should be of coating consistency. Store it as described above.

(3) **Grated Ginger** – After making the ginger pieces, you can grate them and store them as described above. You can use this whenever you need ginger in grated or juliennes form.

Garlic

1. Garlic Flakes

(a) Soak garlic in warm water for some time. It will peel off very easily.

(b) In case of emergency, put your required quantity of garlic on the lid of the pressure cooker to ease peeling.

(c) Place all your bulbs of garlic on the microwave for 30 seconds. Then place them between a rubber garlic peeler or between two rubber/plastic sheets. Rub them lightly for a while. The peels will come off easily. Take some of the peeled garlic and store it in an airtight container. Place it inside the vegetable basket of the refrigerator. This is done to ensure that the smell of raw garlic doesn't spread elsewhere.

(d) While chopping garlic, sprinkle some salt to them. They would neither stick to the chopping board nor the knife.

(e) The best way to keep garlic handy is to peel all the flakes and store in a jar of oil. This oil would be great for salads and tempering.

2. **Garlic Paste** – Make a paste with required amount of water and store in a similar way as ginger paste in the freezer.

Wet and Dry Masalas

1. Soak mustard/poppy seeds/nuts/combination of your choice in a little warm water. You can also soak them in normal water and then warm it in the microwave for 20-30 seconds. Now make a fine paste in a blender adding enough water and a pinch of salt. Add a drop of mustard oil/coconut oil to retain its flavour for a long time. Store this paste in the same manner as ginger paste in the refrigerator.
2. You can always make extra amounts of masalas in advance. Divide the masala into the desired portions according to the recipe. Place the portions in small size containers and freeze till the next time. It is indeed a great time saver.
3. Most of the time people get confused with so many types of masalas because they look similar.

   Example : pav bhaji, sambar, chole or meat masala. The best way to keep a track is to cut the label strips of the masalas and keep it upright in the stored containers. You will never again make mistake in picking the right masala while cooking. If you don't use carton packed masalas, then you can write the name on any piece of paper and cut the strips.

Chicken

1. Although salt increases the water holding capacity of the muscle fibres, resulting in juiciness, marinating the meat with too much of salt before cooking releases the water content, thereby reducing the flavour.
2. While skinning a chicken, peel off a little part of the skin to start with and hold it tightly with a paper towel. The skin latches on to the paper towel and skinning the chicken becomes very easy.

3. To tenderize meat, enzymes play an important role. It can be papain in p:paya/bromolain in Pineapple. It hydrolises the elasticin of the connective tissue.
4. Changing the ph results in hydration and which thereby causes the tenderness and juiciness. This can be done by adding some acidic medium to it like acetic acid in vinegar, citric acid in lemon juice, malic acid in apple (green), tartaric acid in tamarind and raw mango or lactic acid in curd.
5. While buying non-veg items you should make a plan in advance for the smooth running of the week. For example you have bought chicken, bhetki fish, rohu, pomfret and prawns. Let us start with chicken first.

Suppose you have planned to make Indian style chicken curry, chilli chicken, chicken sandwiches, chicken/mix fried rice and chicken soup. Clean and wash the chicken thoroughly. Take out several containers. Refer page no. 89 for 'Grown Up' plastic containers. Divide the chicken in such a way so that you have it for all the recipes.

1. **Chicken Curry**– Marinate this portion with yogurt, ginger - garlic paste, red chilli powder, coriander powder, garam masala and turmeric. Do not put salt now, as it will release all the water content from the chicken. Store it in the usual way in the freezer. Put a label on the top of the container with name of the recipe and date of entry into the freezer. Suppose for in this case the label should read **Chicken curry (18 / 04 /14)**. This helps you to easily identify. which item to use first. When you want to make the curry, take it out in advance from the Freezer and thaw it. Start the show. What are you waiting for? You only have to add brown onion paste, add salt and mix well. Adjust the seasoning. You can add juliennes of bell pepper / tomatoes for a colourful look/simply garnish it with handful of coriander leaves. Since everything

is ready, total preparation time taken should be approximately 15-20 minutes. You can also store the non-veg items without marinating. You can marinate the thawed form & proceed in the suggested way.

2. **Chilli chicken** – Marinate this portion with ginger-garlic paste, juice of one lemon/vinegar, black pepper powder and little soya sauce. Just when you want to cook take this portion in its thawed form. Chop some onion, garlic, celeries (optional) and green chillies and sauté them for a while. Then add the chicken. Adjust your seasoning. Always put lesser amount of salt, as it is already there in soya sauce and Ajinomoto. When almost done add the juliennes of capsicum and chopped spring onion green. When done, add a pinch of Ajinomoto and turn off the flame. You can add a paste of corn flour and water if you want the gravy to be of little thicker consistency. To make it taste like restaurant, fry the chicken pieces (preferably boneless) by slightly coating with cornflour/flour.
3. **Chicken Sandwiches** – While segregating the chicken pieces, keep the menial pieces for sandwiches and soup purpose. You can straight away boil those pieces and shred away flesh and mix with mayonnaise/sandwich spread to make fillings for sandwiches.

   Note: Always put some butter and raw garlic in the water for boiling chicken. This will remove the skunk odour from the chicken.
4. **Chicken/mix Fried Rice** – You can stock small chunk of boneless pieces (either purchased from market or you can make your own boneless ones by cutting small strips of the flesh from the chicken pieces with the help of a kitchen scissor).
5. **Chicken Soup** – Take a few drops of butter/olive oil, add chopped garlic. Sauté it for a while. Add sweet corn / shredded

vegetables (optional). Keep adding stock with bits of shredded chicken, salt, pepper and garnish with chopped spring onion greens. You can serve this for dinner with Garlic bread/normal bread toast. This soup is delicious and healthy. You can also add drops of lemon juice, soya choice, Ajinamoto (optional) for a great taste.

Fish

Fried Fish – Wash and clean the fish. Marinate it with salt and turmeric. Shallow fry them and keep them in the freezer. Whenever you want them with gravy just make the gravy by using your own home made onion paste, ginger paste and garlic paste and tomato puree. Add Masalas according to your taste. Take out the required number of fishes. Put them in the gravy, boil it and add handful of coriander leaves/garam masala powder/ half a cup of yogurt/mustard powder paste. You can use these fried fishes up to a month. Usually frying fish involves oil and grime in the kitchen. It also leaves the kitchen with a skunk odour and visually messy. But here you don't have to face the mess in the kitchen every day. Once done you can clean the kitchen scrupulously with all the suggested technique.

Note: If you want to make any Chinese dishes, fry it with only salt.

Basa/Bhetki fish- Suppose you have planned to make steamed bhetki, chilli fish and fish curry. Clean and wash the fish thoroughly. Take out several containers. Divide the fish in such a way so that you have it in all the recipes.

1. **Fish Fry** –Marinate the fish with salt, ginger and garlic paste, black pepper powder and juice of one lemon. Then dip them in the batter made up of beaten egg, salt and black pepper. Roll it over bread crumbs or crumbled biscuits. You can store

it in this way. You can deep fry now or whenever you need them.

2. **Steamed Bhetki**– Simply marinate the fish with salt and turmeric. Store it in the usual way. Whenever you want to cook this dish, simply thaw the fish. Break some masala paste (coconut, poppy seed, mustard seed and green chillies) of your choice according to your need and add to the fish. Refrigerate for an hour. Add some mustard oil and mix well. Put some whole green chillies and steam it inside a closed steel/aluminium container in the usual way. You can also try the same for Paneer. It really goes well with rice.
3. **Chilli Fish** – Treat this portion in the same way as chilli chicken.
4. **Fish Curry** – Treat this portion in the same way as chicken curry.

Rohu-Suppose you have planned to make fish chop and fish kaliya. Clean and wash the fish thoroughly. Divide the fish in such a way so that you have it for all the recipes.

1. **Fish Chop** – Shallow fry the fish. Debone the fish. Keep it aside and store in the usual way. When you want to make some fish chops, fry some chopped onions till light brown. Add chopped garlic. Fry for a while and then add the fish, boiled and mashed potatoes, seasoning, finely chopped green chillies and coriander leaves. You can also add some raisins if you want. Give them shapes of your choice. Then fry them just like fish fry (discussed above).
2. **Fish Kaliya** – Do the same as you would for fish curry, only make the gravy a bit thicker. Just put more amount of fried onions and whole garam masalas (optional).

Pomfret – Suppose you have planned to make konkani styled fried fish and fish curry. Clean and wash the fish thoroughly.

Divide the fish in such a way so that you have it in all the recipes.

1. **Konkani Styled Fried Fish**– For this portion, marinate the fish with salt, turmeric, ginger and garlic paste, red chilli powder, extract of kokum/tamarind. Now roll it over rawa/ rice flour. You can store them in the usual way in the freezer. When you want to serve, just deep fry them.
2. **Fish Curry** – Same way as for normal fish curries

Prawns - Suppose you have planned to make steamed prawn, prawn cutlet, prawn fried rice and fish curry. Clean and wash the fish thoroughly. Take out several containers. Divide the fish in such a way so that it is in all the recipes.

1. **Steamed Prawn**– Same way as for steamed bhetki.
2. **Prawn Cutlet** – Same method as for fish fry, only difference you have to beat it with the help of a ladle to make it flat.
3. **Prawn Fried Rice/noodles** – Shallow fry them with a little bit of salt and keep aside. Use whenever you want to make noodles/fried rice.
4. **Prawn Masala** – Same as fish kaliya, but this recipe demands the use of liberal amount of coconut. You can always take generous amount of coconut scrapings from the freezer and make a paste along with whole red chillies and then add to the gravy.
5. **Prawn Malai Curry** – In this case simply add coconut milk at the end of the preparation similar to Fish Kaliya. To make coconut milk, simply boil scrapings (full one coconut) in one-two cups of water. Then strain it and use the milk.

Stuffing – If the stuffing consists of meat or fish (example – sautéed with deep fried onions, ginger and garlic), you can store them in an airtight container in the freezer up to one month. Whenever required, take out the container and thaw it to room temperature. Now you have ready to use stuffing which you can use to stuff vegetables like capsicum, tomatoes, potatoes, etc, or use your imagination to make cutlets, chops and bread rolls.

Dry Fruits

1. While using raisins or dry fruits or peels in a cake, first coat them with a little flour and then add to the batter. Then will they not sink to the bottom of the cake. You can also do this to prevent sticking while cutting or chopping them.
2. Always use a scissor to cut and chop them.
3. Chopping becomes much easier if they are placed in the freezer for one hour.
4. Dip nuts in milk before placing them on top of the cakes or biscuits to prevent them from falling off while baking.

Citrus Fruits

1. While buying, opt for large lemons and limes, they tend to be much sweeter. Make sure that the skin is thin, those are much juicer. To obtain more of the juice from lemons, limes or oranges, microwave on high for 30 seconds and then let stand for a couple of minutes before cutting and squeezing.
2. You can also place them in a tumbler filled with lukewarm water. Cover and let the fruits sit on them for a while before making use of them.
3. Pour lemon juice with sugar, salt and a few sprigs of mint (optional) into ice trays, to make cubes which can be used for instant lemonade.

Dal

1. Add a few drops of oil while cooking dals to reduce the cooking time and frothing.
2. To one cup of dal, three-four cups of water are generally added depending on the type of dal.

3. Adding a few fenugreek (methi) seeds to tuvar dal while cooking will make the dal easier to digest.
4. In case of emergency or if you have forgotten to soak Rajma or Chana overnight, soak them in a flask full of boiling water for an hour. They will be ready for cooking.
5. You can cook the 'mother' dal by just boiling it in the cooker with salt and turmeric. Say for example, Arhar (Tur) dal. You can take out half of the amount and store it for second use (b). Now in the same cooker add some chopped vegetables of your choice and give it one whistle. Now you have two options. Either you can make
   (a) **Sambhar** – Add some tamarind extract and sambhar powder. Temper it with mustard seeds, fenugreek seeds, red chillies, curry leaves and a dash of hing. or;
   (b) **Punjabi Style** – Temper it with cumin seeds, mustard seeds. Red and green chillies, hing and ginger-garlic paste. You can add a generous amount of ghee to get a nice aroma.

Soup

1. I personally advice you, never blend any solid ingredients with a good amount of liquid, the former should be drained and pureed separately, the liquid can then be put back into the puree and stirred till it is smooth.
2. To make a clear thin soup, where egg whites is added for globule formation, cook on high flame till it begins to boil stirring all the time so that the egg whites do not get stuck to the base. Then lower the flame and cook without stirring. Strain through a muslin cloth when the raft (solids floating on top) has settled down.

Chappati and Poori

1. While preparing dough, always apply some oil in your hands. It won't stick to your hands.
2. Smear a little bit of oil on the dough. Cover it with a cling film. Store it in an airtight container. You can use this up to a few days. Whenever you require, just take it out by unwrapping the film. You will get freshly made dough.
3. While making chappatis, use hot water to mix the flour. The chappatis will turn out very soft and tasty.
4. The dough should always be kept away covered with a damp muslin cloth for at least half hour after kneading. If chappatis are made immediately, they are not soft.
5. If the freshly made dough is sticking to the rolling pin, keep it in the freezer for one-two minutes.
6. Add a little milk to the dough for fluffier puris.
7. Chapattis would come out very soft if a little rice flour is used while rolling out the dough.
8. While making chapattis, place a kitchen towel under the rolling board. This way the board will not slip and you will be able to roll faster.
9. Try kneading the dough in the milk vessel just before washing. You will get much softer dough and a cleaner utensil.
10. To get a protein rich diet, add half kg of soya bean flour to three kg wheat flour for making nutricious chapatis.
11. Spread a plastic sheet under the rolling board while making chappatis. All the dry flour will fall on the paper and it becomes easy to empty it into the container for re use.
12. For Crispier Puris, add a teaspoon of Semolina/Rava and one teaspoon of Rice flour to the wheat flour while kneading.
13. Try to use ghee instead of oil to the flour while kneading the dough to get extra soft and luscious paranthas.

14. Place rolled puris in the fridge for ten minutes before frying them, they will consume less oil and will be crisper.
15. Any roti or chappati or paratha can be stored in the freezer for upto three months. You can either cook the rotis full or half cook (cook rotis till they are 70 per cent done on both sides) them to recook later before use. Apply ghee/oil/butter whenever needed. Stack them in foil. When reheating, finish cooking rotis on the pan or warm them as instructed.

Storing

Freshly made chapati can be stored in the refrigerator by wrapping stacks of six chapatis in aluminum foil and by placing a wax paper as a separator between the chapatis. This will prevent them from sticking to each other. Then put the foil-stack in a ziplock bag. Let the air out, seal the bag and put it in the freezer. Label each pack with exact numbers of chapattis so that you can plan ahead.

Heating

1. Never reheat chapatis on tava since they become hard after that. Instead wrap them in a clean cloth and put them in an airtight container which fits into your pressure cooker. Cook it for two whistles to make them soft again.
2. Wet a kitchen towel. Squeeze out water. Heat it in the microwave for one minute at high. The kitchen towel will be steaming. Wrap the chapati rolls in the hot kitchen towel and microwave on High for a minute. The lightly moistened kitchen towel ensures proper humidity and prevents the chapati from drying out, or getting chewy.
3. You can also wrap it in cling wrap and microwave for around 30 secs to get softy and warm chapattis.

Buffet Style

The Chapati must remain warm, and not dry-out during party time. Invest in an electric heating pad, stainless steel platters (Thali) and some terrycloth kitchen towels. Lay out the heating pad on the dinner table. Turn it on to 'Low'. Cover heating pad with terrycloth kitchen towels. Place stainless steel platters on the kitchen towels. Place foil wrapped chapati stacks on the stainless steel platters. The heat from heating pad will warm the stainless steel platters through the kitchen towels. The warmed stainless steel platters will keep the double wrapped Chapati stacks (outer wrap of kitchen towel and followed by Aluminum foil wrap) warm. The Aluminum foil will prevent the Chapati from drying out.

Healthy Advices

1. You can also add grated vegetables like carrots, tender white radishes, onions, greens to the flour for making chapatis/ parathas.
2. You can also add besan and any masala like chilli powder, corainder powder, any chopped greens, kasurimethi ... etc; to the flour.
3. There are also several options you can try out if you have a sweet tooth. Make stuffing made up of jaggery and coconut/ crushed peanut/til (sesame seed)/boiled chane ki dal. You can add cardamom powder if you like. Make a potli with your normal Atta dough and stuffing of your choice. Then proceed as usual.
4. You can roll out a large batch of chapatis/ plain parathas/ stuffed parathas/pooris ahead of time and stack with a layer of cling wrap between each (uncooked) chapati/paratha/ poori. Divide into portions as required and store in large, date labelled Ziploc bags/inside a round shaped airtight

container in the freezer. Now you can serve any of the above items any time with ease in a jiffy. Just heat a skillet and roast (for Chapatis), pan-fry (for Parathas) and deep fry (for Puris).

Dosas and Pancakes

1. To ensure that the griddle/tawa is hot enough before spreading dosa, sprinkle a little water over it. If it sizzles immediately, then the griddle is hot enough. Wipe with a clean cloth or half a raw onion and proceed.
2. Try pouring the batter from a used Ketchup bottle to make your dosas and pancakes. Not only you can have control in their size and shape, you will be amazed to see absolutely spotless kitchen counter.
3. Always use silicone brush to apply oil for dosas and pancakes.
4. If dosas stick to the tawa, cut an onion into half. Clean tawa with the cut side of the onion and a little oil. If this does not help, heat tawa empty very well till almost fuming. Switch off the gas. Let it cool. Then reheat and make dosas. Dosas will not stick.
5. To add more flavour and extra crispiness to dosas, add a few fenugreek seeds to the batter.
6. To make neat and crisp dosas, everytime you apply oil on the tawa, sprinkle salt water over it.
7. Add a little sugar to the dosa mixture to make them brown nicely and become crisp.
8. To get light pancakes, add club soda/fruit juice in the batter.

Idlis

1. Add a handful of puffed/crushed rice (chirwa or poha) to the rice while soaking for idlis. You will get fluffier idlis.

2. During winter, add a little fruit salt to the idli batter to make the fermentation faster and idlis softer.
3. The most convenient warm place in which a batter or a dough can rise is the inside of a switched-off oven with the light on.

   Example : Idli, dosa, dhokla, Naan, kulcha, etc.

Pasta and Noodles

1. While boiling pasta and noodles, Drop some oil in the water used for boiling to prevent sticking.
2. If noodles/pasta has to be served later, refresh the boiled noodles in cold water and drain. This way, they will not stick to each other.

Pakoras

1. Add a handful of puffed/crushed rice (chirwa or poha)/rice flour/cornflour to the pakora batter for extra crisp pakoras.
2. The batter should be beaten well with hand to incorporate air in the batter thereby making it light.
3. To test if the consistency of your wada batter is correct, drop a little batter into a cup of water. If it floats it is ready to be fried.
4. Adda pinch of salt to the oil. This is because impurities in the salt tend to draw the moisture content thus making your pakoras draw less oil.

Chops/Cutlets

1. For getting a thick, crisp coating on cutlets or rolls, dip the prepared snack in egg white beaten with a few Tablespoon of water and then roll in fine bread crumbs. For vegetarians, you can dip them in a thin batter of maida and water and then roll in bread crumbs. Fry till well browned.
2. In the absence of bread crumbs, semolina /suji/rice flour/

powdered sago may be used to get a thin, yet crisp coating. Crushed vermicelli will give a nest-like appearance.

3. If the chops/cutlets develop cracks, add some bread soaked in water for a second and then drained, to the cutlet mixture.

Sandwiches

1. Wrap sandwiches without cutting the sides, in foil or cling wrap to keep them soft. Cut the crust only at the time of serving to prevent the edges from drying.

   Zest - Zest or grated peel of lemon, lime or orange can be added to sauces, cakes, puddings, soufflés, cookies or even marinades for an extra tangy flavour.

Green Leaves

1. Remove the string which is tied to hold them. Clean (without water) and remove the unwanted parts. Chop them into required sizes. Store it in plastic kitchen bags for future use.
2. Use kitchen scissors to trim fresh mint, basil, cilantro leaves and chilies finely without any mess. Whenever you need it for garnishing purpose, take a handful in a strainer, wash them under running water and sprinkle them over the dish. Use it within a week.
3. To clean the leaves if you need in larger amount (for chutney/ gravy purpose), plunge them into a sink full or pot full of cold water. Swirl around a few times and let it sit for a while. The sand, dirt, and other debris will settle to the bottom, and the leaves will float to the top and can be removed. Repeat the procedure if they are very dirty.
4. Do not rinse them until just before using. As soon as you bring cilantro home from the market, keep it upright in a glass of warm water to give it a final drink. Then wrap a wet paper towel around its roots and store in the vegetable crisper

drawer in case you don't have the time to immediately chop them.

5. You can also fill each cube in an ice cube tray with the finely chopped cilantro or mint leaves (cleaned and washed). Top each cube with cold water and freeze. The cilantro or mint cubes can be dropped into curries, etc., as and when required. You can also store freshly cut herbs (parsley, celery, etc.) in this way.

Milk

Milk is not a simple liquid. It is a colloid. It contains large quantity of water and many substances (protein, sugar and fat) in suspended form. When milk is heated slowly, first, the proteins and fat get separated. Since fat is lighter than milk, they collect on the surface in the form of a layer called cream. Second, some water gets converted into water vapour which being lighter, rises up. As the upper layer of the milk is covered with cream, the vapour gets trapped below it. On further heating, this vapour expands and thick foam is produced on top. Finally, the trapped vapour pushes itself through the cream layer and bursts resulting in the spilling of milk as well as cream.

To Prevent Milk from Spilling

1. Keep a long-handled spoon in the milk container to enable the water vapour to escape along the handle of the spoon.
2. Before pouring milk into a pot for boiling rub butter along the top edge and inside lip of the pot. When the milk foams up, it will stop over spilling when it hits the butter.
3. Always stir milk with a wooden spoon while making custards or kheer, and keep the flame low after it boils.

   Note: While stirring try making a figure of "8" for even mixing.

4. To reduce the time in kheer making, add sugar only after the rice is done.

Butter

1. To get an exact measure, cut a slice of one cm, and then divide it into four pieces, each piece would be a table spoon.
2. While using butter for cooking, add little oil to it to prevent it from getting burnt.

Cream

1. To get thick cream, cover the milk vessel with a thin muslin cloth and refrigerate overnight.
2. Never overdo your whipping, otherwise butter will form. Always whip over a tray or a large tumbler filled with ice cubes. Whip in sharp upward strokes till soft peak form. Keep in refrigerator till used.
3. While whipping, do not add sugar at the beginning because it will result in lower volume. Add sugar when it is almost done to obtain a higher volume.
4. Make homemade sour cream by adding one teaspoon of lemon juice to every half pint of fresh cream and stir. Keep it aside for fifteen minutes before using it.

Paneer

1. While making paneer from milk, don't throw away the whey (paneer water). This nutritious water can be used for making soft dough for chapatis or can be used to cook dals.
2. For Indian dishes, there is no need for frying paneer at all. You can boil some water with a little pinch of salt and turmeric. When the water is at full boil, you can put the paneer and put the flame off. When your masala for the paneer is ready, just drain the paneer pieces and put them in the gravy. Don't keep them for more than one boil.

3. To keep the paneer soft and luscious after deep frying, dip it in lukewarm water in which a pinch of salt is added. This is essential while making chilli/Manchurian/sweet and sour paneer.

Curd

1. Don't throw away the whey which is obtained after making hung curd. Use it to knead your atta dough.
2. To prevent curdling, add salt to the curd based gravy only after curd is cooked.
3. To set thick curd, add little cornflour paste into the milk while setting.
4. Make curd in cold weather by setting it inside a casserole/ microwave (light on).
5. When adding curd to curries, always remember to beat the curd. Remove the pan from fire when adding the curd or milk to the masala. Stir well to mix. Return to low heat.

Eggs

1. You don't have to buy an expensive egg yolk separator. You can use a funnel to separate the yolk from the white. Break the eggs inside the funnel. The white will pass through and the yolk will remain in the funnel.
2. For those using only egg whites, you can store the egg yolks in a bowl with some milk, to use it for making omlette later for the kids.
3. To beat the egg whites light as air, they should be at room temperature while beating.
4. To ease cutting/slicing of hard boiled eggs, keep them in the refrigerator for some time.
5. Scrambled eggs should be served immediately after cooking. Never reheat them directly, use the double boiling technique

instead to maintain its softness. On heating while making them, coagulation of proteins takes place. This on further heating causes the product to shrink and become dry.

Rice

1. Wash the rice a few times until the water runs clear. Remove all the water until no water remains. Let it sit for 20 minutes. This will remove all the starch and help the grains to remain separate.
2. While cooking rice add a few drops of lemon juice to retain the whiteness of the grains.
3. Refrigerate leftover cooked rice in a well-sealed container. Reheat cold rice with a sprinkling of water in a microwave oven or in a covered pot over low heat.
4. Leftover cooked rice can be the best alternative to noodles and pasta which can be thrown over any hot soups.

Potato/Banana Wafers

1. For making potato chips/crispy alu bhajiya, soak the potatoes in ice cold water for an hour. Then deep fry them to make them crispier. Add salt only after that.
2. To get extra crisp chips, sprinkle the soaked, dried chips with some flour before frying. Maida absorbs any excess water present.
3. To get crispy French fries, deep-fry them till half done. Cool and then store in an airtight container/zip lock bag in freezer. Re fry them before serving.
4. You can store fried papads and chips fresh and crispby putting them in a polythene bag and store them in a refrigerator.
5. Reduce boiling time of potatoes by putting a little vinegar to the water.

6. You can store boiled potatoes in the refrigerator up to three days by storing them in their jackets or by putting them in cold water to which a few drops of vinegar have been added. You can make use of the potato anytime you want to (in making stuffing for pani puri, alu kabli, chaat, alu tikiya, etc.)

Spices

1. Always add freshly grated nutmeg only at the end of cooking as heat diminishes its unique flavour.
2. Never add saffron directly to a dish, soak the threads in a bowl of hot water or warm milk for at least five minutes before blending it in a dish to bring out the perfect aroma.
3. Never fry saffron in hot oil or butter, as the heat will ruin the flavour.
4. Ground spices tend to lose their natural flavour within a short span of time. Try to use them within two months. For black pepper, it is advisable to use it within a week.

Salad

1. Always use wooden/glass bowl to toss salad. Also try to use a wooden spoon.
2. Lettuce should always be hand torn since it gets discoloured when cut with a knife.
3. Never forget to sprinkle some salt, sugar or lime juice over cut apples to prevent discoloration.
4. Make salad dressing in a jiffy by blending a cup of hung curd, one tsp of lime juice, 1tsp of olive oil and seasoning and toss the salad into it.
5. If you are to use lettuce for salad decoration for any party, always line the salad tray with silver foil with a layer of ice cubes beneath it. Now decorate your salad on the bed of

lettuces according to your choice. The lettuces will stay fresh and will not become shabby.

6. Acid has strong impact on chlorophyll. The acid's hydrogen atom replaces the magnesium in chlorophyll, turning the colour to a yellowish grey green. This is why green vegetables turn drab if they stand in a tart dressing for more than a few minutes. To minimise the colour change, dress vegetables just before serving.

Chocolate

Double Boiling

It is a technique in which eggs and other heat-sensitive items such as chocolates, sauce, custards are heated for cooking purpose slowly and evenly, eliminating the possibility of scorching or overcooking. Direct heat causes those delicate substances to break down, thus ruining their consistency.

Double Boiler

A double boiler is a specialised equipment consisting of two fitted saucepans. The larger saucepan partially filled with water is brought to a simmer or boil. The inner saucepan uses this indirect heat to melt chocolate, cook custards, sauces and wax for candle making. You can also use a large saucepan and a bowl, in case you don't possess one.

Process

Fill the bottom of double boiler with water and place on low heat.

1. Place coarsely chopped chocolate in the top of double boiler over hot water and allow it to melt. Do not cover.
2. Keep stirring until smooth.
3. Remove the chocolate bowl/top of the boiler from heat.

4. Utmost care should be taken at the time of melting. If any drop of water accidentally fall into the chocolate, the process will stop and the chocolate will stiffen and solidify.
5. Use the above technique if you are making chocolate icing cake.

Sauce

1. To get a smooth texture of sauce, you can run it in the food processor for a minute. You can add desired amount of water.
2. While cooking **White Sauce**, try placing half of an onion wrapped around with a bay leaf and fixed together with a clove. These three ingredients will enhance the flavour as well as absorb the raw smell of flour.
3. Another thing which I normally do is to fry White flour in butter and store it in airtight container in the refrigerator. Then use it to make white sauce in a similar manner of making custard.
4. Proportion should be one tsp of flour per one cup of milk. Suppose you have to make two cups of the sauce. Take two tsps of that flour in a cup and add a little milk and mix to form a smooth paste. Once the milk (two cups) is boiled, you can add this paste slowly.
5. Always remember to remove the pan from fire when adding the paste for making white sauce/custard. Stir well to mix. Return to low heat and gradually on high, stirring continuously till it thickens. You can also add a little amount of water (optional).
6. Use the above technique for making Chinese gravies. Whatever amount of liquid you want to keep in the dish, keep it. Slowly add the corn-flour paste in the manner mentioned above. Never put extra water after it is cooked. It spoils the taste of the gravy.

Vegetables

(i) Tips for Cooking Vegetables

1. Cooking time should be reduced to prevent the vegetables from becoming bland and mushy and also loss of vitamins and minerals.
2. Cut vegetables into similar-sized pieces to ensure even cooking.
3. Herbs and delicate spices lose their flavour if it is added in the beginning of the cooking.
4. Use a small amount of water to cook fibrous vegetables. Fresh vegetables often do not need any water, as too much water increases cooking time, resulting in loss of nutrients. It is not necessary to add water to frozen vegetables.
5. Vegetables that grow above ground should be cooked uncovered.
6. Vegetables that grow underground should be cooked covered.
7. A teaspoon of sugar can be added to remove bitterness from fenugreek leaves when the latter is almost cooked.
8. Since sugar is a very good preservative, it retains the flavour of almost all the vegetables when the latter is cooked with a pinch of it.
9. Cauliflower florets should always be soaked in warm salted water for a while to get rid of any tiny insects that may be present deep inside the florets which are not visible to the naked eye.
10. To retain the golden yellow colour of American sweet corn, one teaspoon of lemon juice should be added to the water in which it is cooked just a minute before removing from heat. Salt should not be put while cooking corn, because it only toughens the corn.

11. To get a golden glaze as well as an enhanced flavour to any dish, you can try adding a small amount of sugar, honey or any fruit juice just before the cooking is almost done.
12. If the vegetables are not appearing fresh according to your benchmark, soak them in cold water to which a little lemon juice has been added.
13. Strong flavored vegetables like cabbage, cauliflower, onions, etc. should be cooked uncovered so that the flavour may be decreased by evaporation.
14. Cover the food during cooking on griller to retain the moisture/juice which otherwise would have evaporated.
15. Adding a tablespoon of curd/a teaspoon of lemon juice while cooking ladies fingers will prevent them from sticking.
16. To get a flavour of methi in any gravy, take a small ball of dough and roll it over some methi seeds. Fry this in plain oil. Remove and throw it away when it turns into golden brown. Use this oil for cooking. You can also boil this dumpling in any gravy and later throw it away to get a subtle flavor of methi but at the same time, it will never come into your bite. You can try the same for whole garam masalas (cloves, cinnamon, cardamoms, peppercorns, star-anise, etc.) also.
17. Another thing which I normally do is boiling those ingredients which are not liked by my family members (like whole spices/bay leaf/curry leaves/methi seeds) in water and then pour it in the required gravy/pulao/halwa/upma after straining it.
18. To get homemade veg/non veg food even after coming from vacation/after a hectic day at the hospital. Just chill...... Get the required stuff from the freezer. If you have time, you can leave it for a few hours and after thawing just give it a boil

with some water (tip no. 17) and garnish with freshly chopped coriander or green chilli. If you don't have the time, defrost it in the machine. You can also add ghee/kasuri methi/ whatever.

19. Sprinkle little bit of gram flour over the vegetables while frying to absorb the excess oil as well as making the vegetable tastier.
20. Adding cold water to overcooked meat and vegetables will considerably harden them a bit.
21. Soak 1-2 tbsp of cashew nuts or almonds or magaz (watermelon seeds) or chironji. Grind them to a fine paste before adding to your gravy. It will thicken as well as enhance flavour to the gravy.
22. Concentration of acids is lower in vegetables then in fruits. Low acids means high ph value

(ii) When to Add Salt to the Vegetables

For most of the vegetables, (beans, peas, bottle gourd, ridge gourd, cabbage and other leafy vegetables) salt should only be added after they are almost cooked. This is because they tend to release high amount of water.

Exception

1. While cooking soup, stews and sauces, salt should be added in the beginning. Here it is desirable to draw out the flavour of the vegetables and blend in the liquid smoothly and evenly.
2. While boiling potatoes, add the salt to the water as potatoes absorb salt better this way.

(iii) Different Methods for Cooking Vegetables)

1. **Boiling**

Boiling consists of putting the vegetables in boiling water and cooking them at simmer. Cover vegetables while cooking to reduce cooking time and the evaporation of volatile substances. Boiling significantly reduces the flavour and nutritional value of vegetables. Use only a small amount of water and reserve the cooking liquid for making dals or to knead your atta dough.

2. **Steaming**

   Steaming consists of using the heat released from a small amount of boiling water. Place vegetables in a single layer in a steamer or steam basket just one inch (2.5 cm) above the simmering water. Add the vegetables to the steamer only when the water starts to boil. Cover. When the lid releases steam, lower the heat to keep the water just at simmering point. Time taken for steaming vegetables is longer but there is less loss of nutrients and flavour.

   You can also make modaks, momos or pulis (sweet dumplings) by lining them in a steam basket. Then put it over a kadai/half filled with water and cover it with a lid.

3. **Pressure-Cooking**

   Pressure-cooking consists of cooking within an airtight container. Since the temperature in the pressure cooker rises above boiling point, the non-veg, vegetables cook very rapidly. You can use it to cook caramel pudding, idli, dhokla, etc.

4. **Quick-braising**

   This involves cooking vegetables in their own juice after sautéeing in a small amount of fat or oil. A small amount of liquid (water, wine, tomato sauce, cooking juices, etc.) can be added at the beginning to get the process started. Cover and cook over low heat to blend flavors well. This goes with vegetables like squash, mushrooms, tomatoes, onions and shallots.

5. **Braising**

   Braising consists of cooking foods slowly, covered, over a low heat, after sautéing in fat or oil. Cook vegetables whole or in pieces. Vegetables can be braised by themselves or with a pieces of meat/prawn to create tasty combinations. This goes with harder vegetables like artichoke, cabbage, celery, etc.

6. **Dry-heat Cooking**

   This method uses the heat from an oven (grilling)or barbecue. Vegetables can be cooked whole with their skin or cut into pieces. This goes with vegetables like egg plant, tomatoes and potato where their skin has to be pricked so that they don't burst from internal pressure. This method makes vegetables tender, juicy and tasty, and restricts the loss of nutrients. You can also prick brinjal with chillies, garlic, etc., and dry roast it over slow flame.

7. **Stir-frying**

   Stir-frying makes use of a light, quick frying or steaming process, or a combination of the two. Group vegetables according to their cooking time and fry them quickly in oil over a very high heat, beginning with those requiring the longest cooking time. Aromatic vegetables like shallots, leek, galangal, ginger, garlic, green chili, kafir lime leaves or zest of any citrus fruit can be added (optional). A small amount of liquid like water blended with cornstarch, sauce, stock, etc., can also be added. This method goes with firmer vegetables such as cauliflower, broccoli and carrots.)

8. **Deep-frying**

   Deep-frying consists of cooking at high temperature by immersing food in oil/ghee. They can be fried directly/after dipping in flour, beaten egg and bread crumbs. They should be drained and blotted on paper towel to absorb excess oil.

9. **Microwaving**

   It utilises ultrasound waves in a specially designed oven. Details are given separately latter.

(iv) Blanching and Freezing of Vegetables

Most vegetables (except those with high acidic content) need to be blanched before frozen. Place the vegetables in a metal basket or a steamer. Immerse the vegetables only when the water is at full boil. Cover and start timing the blanching process. While **Blanching** vegetables, they should be kept in the hot water just long enough to slightly soften and then immediately placed inside cold water to ensure a crisp texture. Drain the vegetables and seal in freezer bags, squeezing out all of the air. Quantity and the date of freezing the vegetables should be written on the freezer bag. Vegetables can generally be stored in a freezer for up to one year. The cooking time for frozen vegetables is shorter than fresh vegetables as the vegetables have already been partly cooked during the blanching process.

(v) Science behind the Colour of the Vegetables

Generally in the first phase, hot water, steam, or fat, causes green vegetables to become brighter, but with longer cooking the green fades. Heat causes the gases surrounding the vegetable cells to expand and escape. As a result the green pigment chlorophyll can be seen more clearly. Same thing happens with **Stir–fried vegetables** where cooking is done so quickly, they stay quite green if eaten hot. Same for **Boiled/Steamed/ Microwaved vegetables** like green beans, peas, asparagus, broccoli, cabbage, and leafy become tender and crisp enough to be eaten while still keeping their bright colours. If the vegetables have to be reheated later, drain the vegetables and immerse them in ice water until cool. This stabilises the chlorophyll and arrests the colour change. When reheated, the vegetables won't fade as rapidly as during first cooking. That is why frozen green vegetables keep their colour longer when cooked. On further heating, colour of the vegetables eventually turns to greyish yellow, as heat displaces the magnesium atoms in the chlorophyll, responsible for the change in colour.

The bright colour of the vegetables and fruits is mainly due to the many **Pigments** it contains. The green colour of vegetables is attributed to the **Green plant pigment Chlorophyll**. There is a magnesium ion in the centre of the chlorophyll molecule. Vegetables contain several **Organic Acids**, which decrease the pH level of the cooking water and displace the magnesium ion from the chlorophyll molecule. The **Alkaline Baking soda** (sodium bicarbonate) **neutralises the acids** in vegetables and thus prevent the displacement of the magnesium ion from the chlorophyll molecule. In this way, the vegetables **retain their bright green colour**.

(I) Water Insoluble Pigments

One such is **Chlorophyll a,** the most dominating of all is bluish green in colour. Other is **Cartenoid** responsible for the bright colours like yellow, red, orange as in the case of carrot, red pepper, corns. Another one is **Chlorophyll b**, a dull yellow green colour pigment.

Water Soluble Pigment

Flavanoids in the form of **Anthocyanins** (red to purple) impart colour to fruits and vegetables like cherries, berries, grapes, pomgrenates, radish, sweet potatoes and red cabbage and **Antho xanthins** (colourless, pale yellow or white) responsible for the colour in cauliflower and onions.

Earlier **Copper coins and unlined copper pans** were used

for cooking to retain the colour of the vegetables. Free copper or zinc ions contained in those vessels, replaced magnesium in chlorophyll, giving the green colour a bluish ting.

(vi) How to Retain the Colour of the Vegetables

1. Greens should never be overcooked since they lose their colour, taste and vital nutrients.
2. Green vegetables should be cooked uncovered, otherwise the acids they contain become concentrated and destroy their chlorophyll, which makes them lose their colour. Also it helps in eliminating some volatile acids.
3. While cooking Greens like beans and Brocolli, sprinkle a pinch of baking soda to help retain the colour of greens since alkaline ingredient preserves their colour.
4. To retain the colour of your **Green chutney** for a long time, add a handful of boondis to the blender while making it. The soda content in the boondis will help in retaining the colour.
5. To retain the whiteness in cauliflower, add some milk during cooking. It enhances taste as well. You can do the same while cooking Eggplants to prevent them from becoming black.
6. Adding an acidic ingredient (vinegar, citrus juice, dry wine, cider), changes the ph level of the liquid in which it is cooked. This helps in preserving the colour and firmness of red (red cabbage, red pepper) and white vegetables.

(vii) How to make the most of your Valuable Time

1. **Cut Vegetables**– Store vegetables in whichever way you want to, be it chopped, diced or shredded. My advice is to use food processor for one day and get optimum results.
2. Suppose you have **planned the week's menu** consisting of sambhar (which requires chopped mix vegetables).

Mix Vegetable–which requires chopped mix vegetables.

Carrot/Lauki halwa–which requires grated carrots/Lauki.

Vegetable kofta–which requires grated vegetable mix and cabbage.

Chinese Noodles–which requires shredded carrots, capsicums, beans and onions.

Muli Paratha–grated radish.

Except for salads and onions, you can save a lot of time by diligently planning, cutting, shredding, dicing, etc., the vegetables according to your need. Store everything in plastic bags or Tupperware container in your refrigerator (if you want to use for a week). Store it in the freezer (if you want to use it for a month).

3. **Sautéed Sabzis** – In Indian cuisine we also have a lot of side dishes where we don't require rich gravy, e.g., avial (a dish from South India), shukto, lauki, mulor chechki (from West Bengal) curry (from Gujarat), gatti ki sabzi (from Rajasthan), etc. These dishes can be three fourth cooked and kept in the refrigerator. You can make these dishes in a jiffy when you have a grand feast at home.

   Avial – You can boil the vegetables and mix it with a paste made up of coconut and yogurt. Now keep this in an airtight container. Just before serving you can temper it with south Indian whole spices.

   Shukto – Boil the vegetables with a little bit of grated ginger. Store this in the usual way. Just before serving temper it with Bengali five spice mix/mustard and fenugreek. You can also add a paste of poppy seeds/mustard mixed with a little bit of coconut scrapings.

   Lauki – Sauté the vegetable with salt and turmeric till it is done. Store this in the usual way. Just before serving, temper it with mustard seeds / cumin seeds, grated ginger green chillies, handful of chopped coriander leaves. You can also add freshly fried vadis / fried shrimps to give it an authentic taste.

Mulor Chechki – Sauté the grated muli with salt and turmeric till it is done. Cooking style is similar to that of the lauki.

Curry – Make a smooth batter with gram flour, yogurt, salt and turmeric. Store this in the usual way. It should be thinner than dropping consistency. You can also make pakoras in advance with onions/palak and onion/methi and onion with a pinch of baking soda. Store this in airtight containers. Just before serving, simmer the batter. When it begins to boil, dip the pakoras inside. Temper with hing, cumin seeds, mustard seeds, ginger - garlic paste and slit green chillies.

Gatti ki Sabzi – You can prepare gattis in advance and store them. Follow the above steps to make its curry.

Tomatoes

1. To peel tomatoes easily, place them in boiling water for a few seconds. Add a little sugar when cooking tomatoes to bring out their flavour and to cut acidity.
2. **Tomato Puree** – Boil some amount of water. Blanch the tomatoes. Blend it to make a fine puree. Now store it into airtight containers of smaller size in the freezer. Whenever you require any gravy or tomato soup, your readymade puree is at your service. Just take out one small container and thaw it to room temperature. It requires approximately two hours. If you have an emergency you can defrost it in a microwave or place the container in a tumbler filled with warm water.
3. Alternatively, you can also spoon tomato puree into ice cube trays. Freeze overnight. Transfer into plastic bags and freeze. Frozen cubes can be dropped right into **curries/soup**. Same

way you can do with **Tamarind pulps** and the frozen cubes of **Tamarind extracts** can be thrown directly into **Sambar, Rasam and chutneys.**

4. Dip overripe tomatoes in cold water, add some salt and leave them overnight. They will be fresh and firm to touch the next day.
5. Always remember to continue frying tomatoes or its puree till the oil separates before adding curd or milk to the gravy. This will prevent the milk/curd from curdling.

   Green Peas – Remove the pea shells. Put the peas in a large pan of boiling water, keep it for a while. Put off the heat and take the peas out. Cool them and keep them in zip lock bag.

   Green Chilli – Trim the end and store them in an airtight container.

Sugar Syrup

Always add a few drops of lemon juice while preparing sugar syrup. The impurities will collect on the surface of the syrup, which can be removed afterwards.

Mushroom

When sautéing fresh mushrooms, sprinkle with a little lemon juice to prevent discoloration.

Remedy for Salty Curry

1. Wash a potato. Cut into two. Place the two halves of the raw potato in the curry and it will absorb the extra salt.
2. You can make a few small atta dough balls and put them in the gravy. Boil it and let them remain for some time in the curry. Remove them just before serving.
3. If accidentally, the curry turned to be a bit oily and pungent, take two bread slices and crumble them coarsely. Add this to the curry and mix well. Bread absorbs the excess oil and spice.

Different types of flour– It is again confusing when it comes to identify rice flour, wheat flour or corn flour. You can use my technique of using strips of paper with proper names written on them.

Important Tips for Baking the Perfect Cake

1. Always measure the ingredients with great precision. Using the correct amounts of ingredients are more important than the beating of the cakes. Don't hesitate to buy a measuring cup and a measuring spoon from a good supermarket. This is more than necessary.
2. Fill the cake tin three/four with cake batter, allowing space for cake to rise.
3. The art of making good cakes also lies in beating the mixture till it becomes light and fluffy.
4. Always sieve the baking powder with the flour at the time of making the cake.
5. In the presence of heat and moisture, the baking powder reacts to form carbon dioxide gas in a baked product to make it rise.
6. Never use baking powder which is more than a year old.
7. Always preheat the oven at the temperature at which you have to bake your cake for at least 10 minutes.
8. Always grease your baking tin and dust (sprinkle) with flour.
9. To prevent white streaks in the chocolate cake, sprinkle the greased cake tin with cocoa instead of flour.
10. Baking should always be done in aluminium or anodised containers.
11. Do not open the oven door again and again to check the cake as this causes variation in the temperature and hence affects the baking.

12. Test your cake with a clean knife at the place where the cake has risen the most, i.e. at the highest point, before removing from the oven.
13. Permit the cake to cool for sometime before you remove it from the tin.
14. Never cool a cake under the fan as this will make the cake dry and hard.
15. Tip on using the butter in baking mixtures meant for pie crust/tart. Take some flour and several cubes of butter in one hand and coat the butter cubes with the flour. Flatten the cubes a bit while rubbing the flour across it till they are all broken up. Now make a well in the center of your dry ingredients and add the wet ingredients. Always use a fork to toss together the two mixtures. Sweep the fork along the sides of the bowl, tossing the dry into the wet and gradually folding/mixing lightly. When it has barely come together, use your hands to knead it until just combined. Never over mix them otherwise they would result in gluten formation. Cover it with cling flim/plastic wrap and keep them inside the fridge for half an hour. Then take it out, roll it out lightly on a lightly floured surface and cut into cookies/biscuits. Brush with egg whites and bake for 10 minutes.
16. Soften your dry cakes by brushing them with milk and warming them in the oven for a couple of minutes.
17. You can prevent drying of a cake by placing 1/2 apple in the cake box or, if a slice of fresh bread is fastened with toothpicks to the cut edge of the cake.

Bread

1. To soften as well as refresh leftover hardened bread, place them on the lid of a pan containing hot water.

2. To refresh stale bread/bun/rolls, sprinkle a little milk/water over it and place it in a moderately hot oven for a few minutes.
3. Cut fresh bread with a hot knife.
4. Leftover dry breads can be used to make bread crumbs and store them in the freezer.

Rawa

1. Roast the rawa with ghee or white oil till the aroma starts wafting. Store it in an air tight container. You can keep it outside in a dry place.
2. **For Halwa Purpose** – Whenever you want to make halwa, take a pan, pour some water in it. Put some sugar and cardamom into it. When the mixture starts to boil, put the roasted rawa onto it and stir it continuously till the halwa is done. You can also mix some dry fruits/coconut scrapings (optional). This way you can make delicious halwa in about five minutes approximately.

   Note: The proportion of water should be 2.5 times that of the rawa.
3. **For upma purpose** – Take some oil in a pan. Put mustard seeds, Bengal gram daal, red chillies. When they begin to splutter, add curry leaves. You can also add some coconut scrapings. Add seasoning and sauté them till they are done. Whenever you want to make upma, do the above (halwa) procedure. Only instead of adding dry fruits, add some sautéed vegetables and mix well and serve it hot or pack it for tiffin.

   Coloured Ice – Make some squashes with the readymade Rasana/Kissan fruit squash. Pour them into ice trays. After they set, take out the coloured ice cubes and store them in plastic bags. During summer, serve soft drinks with this coloured ice cubes in them to your guests. It will be a delight to see a spectrum of colours mingling with one another.

Point to Remember – I am sharing my time tested tricks and short cut methods with you to save your time and effort. You need not follow my instructions blindly, rather I would suggest use it according to your convenience, specific need and taste.

Example: If you have high **BP patient** at home. You should first cook food which you want to give him, i.e., with less oil and with almost no seasoning. Then you can separately add seasoning, red chilli powder and more oil/ghee to the remaining portion.

Suppose you have **diabetes patient** at home. Same rules should be followed while putting sugar to your food.

When there are **small kids** at home. If you don't have enough time to cook separately, prepare a basic meal which does not consist of any of the following-green chillies, red chillies, herbs, juliennes, garnishes like cilantro, coriander or curry leaves, sauces, powdered spices, etc.

Instead use dollops of ghee because that will give necessary benefits to their health. For adults, they can add whatever they want to the dish as per their requirement.

A little compromise is sure to have an everlasting effect on your personal and family life in the long run. You can spend that extra time with your near and dear ones or maybe catch up with your old pals for a movie/a chat over a cup of coffee. You can also start pursuing your old hobby or a new passion you have just discovered. A little planning goes a long way!

So Celebrate Your Life!

2

How to Make

1. **Flavoured Tea** – If you love the fragrance of rose/jasmine you can store their petals in the same container in which you have stored tea. You can also sun dry some orange peel or ginger flakes and then add it to the tea container.
2. **Hung Curd** – Take a muslin cloth and place the yogurt in it, tie it up and place it on top of a colander in such a way that the whey will drain out naturally. To prevent both the yogurt and the whey from getting sour, it is to best to place the colander inside the refrigerator overnight. You can use the whey to make atta dough; it contributes valuable proteins to the dough.
3. **Defrost Naturally** – Whatever you want to defrost, just take it out of the freezer a few hours before and allow it to defrost naturally by keeping in the fridge.

3

How To

1. **Wash Whites** – To get a dazzling white look for your white clothes, always remember you have to pre-treat the clothes.
2. **Hand Washing** – First soak the clothes in Bleach solution overnight. In the morning, wash them with plain water and then soak them in a solution of detergent and few drops of liquid blue. Wash them in the usual way, making an extra effort to scrub the collars and the cuffs with washing soap bar and a cloth brush.
3. For **PT Uniform or Other Sportswear**, if the uniform gets soiled with mud and sticky dirt, soak them in a bucket of cold water and wash thoroughly with enough cold water to get rid of the mud and dirt. Scrub the stained parts with soap bar and cloth brush before soaking in hot water and repeat the above mentioned said steps.

   Note: Never soak them directly in warm water, as they would dye the muddy stain onto the clothes.

   (a) For **white socks**, try to pile them up and soak them in a solution of bleach and detergent. Then wash them with a bar soap by hand and not with a brush. Otherwise the stain gets in to the sock and it is very difficult to remove them.

   (b) **Automatic Washing Machine** – Soak the white clothes in a solution of bleach and water overnight. In the morning wash the clothes in plain water and put them in the washing machine with adequate amount (as required by the machine) of detergent. You can add a few drops of blue while washing if you desire to give the clothes a dazzling look. If the machine has an option for hot wash, opt for it. Otherwise take the pain to pour some lukewarm water. Try not to add non-white clothes. This will ensure that the white remains white. I advise you to pile up your white clothes and do the laundry.

Note: Here, you have to scrub the stained parts with bar and a brush before you put them inside the washing machine.

(c) **Semi Automatic Washing Machine** – In this type of machine there are advantages as well as disadvantages. Here follow the same steps as you would for automatic machine. Only added advantage is that you can recycle your detergent solution up to three times. First time starts with your whites. Second it can be any light colour clothes and third time it can be clothes of darker shade.

Note: Here, you have to scrub the stained parts with bar and a brush after it is washed and then rinse it off with clean cold water.

2. Arrange Wardrobes

The prime reason for most of the rooms looking messy and untidy is because arrangement of this part of your belongings is never planned for. It is the most neglected areas in several homes. Wardrobes are generally bought readymade, hence, is not customised to your needs.

You should try to invent new tips every now and then in keeping your wardrobe organised. A well organised wardrobe not only boosts the aesthetics of a home but is a stress buster and a great time saver.

Technique

(i) With a little bit of imagination you can create enough space in your wardrobe to fit all the clothes and accessories.

(ii) Devote at least half an hour every week to maintain your wardrobe. This is very important. Otherwise you are bound to face Tsunami in the time of your need.

(iii) You should always have separate shelves for separate items in your wardrobe. For example keep the winter and summer garments separately. There are different techniques of storing each type. Try to follow them in order to keep your garments fresh and new for long.

(iv) You should also segregate your clothes based on their conditions and priorities. Do not keep the regular or casual wears with that of the special ones. This might ruin them. Be careful while storing your high value garments. It is advisable to hang them in your wardrobe as this will keep them in good shape.

(v) Many of our clothing items do not require a wash for a long time if worn properly.

Example: Expensive silks, cotton handloom type sarees, formal wear salwar kameezes, etc. Have a good shower, don't forget to put on a deodorant and then simply wear them for an occasion or work place. Take care not to spoil your attire. Always keep some wet tissue in your hand bag. After you come home, you can let it dry for a while and iron your garments properly for further use. This will keep them in good condition for long and they won't loose their lustre due to repeated washing.

(vi) Due to lack of storage space, we sometimes tend to keep our stock of upholstery like linens, furnishings, towels, etc. in our wardrobe. This unnecessarily tends to put pressure on your delicate fabrics and spoil it. Try to avoid it.

Techniques in Arranging the Wardrobe

Male

(i) You can arrange your garments by hanging your clothes according to type, length and colour.

Example: Shirts and trousers first. You can arrange the shirts and trousers according to colour (from light to dark shades) or according to sleeves (short sleeve first and long sleeve shirts last). Same thing goes with hanging T–shirts, kurtas, etc.

(ii) You can hang the suits on the right side of the closet on special hangers (plastic/wooden ones). These gives better support to them, especially, at the shoulders.

(iii) Shirts, T-shirts, kurtas can be neatly folded and kept in the shelves if you don't have adequate space to hang them.

(iv) Last grouping will consist of vests, undergarments, socks, handkerchiefs, ties and belts. For the handkerchiefs, you can simply fold them and keep in piles in a utility basket/in a tray and store it in any vacant space available in your wardrobe. You can also store it in any utility drawers if you have one with pen, glasses, sunglasses, mobiles, etc.

Female

(i) You can arrange by hanging your clothes according to type, length and colour or from shorter to longer items.

Example: Arrange sarees first, then the fancy tops and trousers according to colour (from light to dark shades) or sleeves (sleeveless first and long sleeves at the last). Same thing goes with hanging T– shirts, kurtas, etc. This is only possible if you have adequate space in your wardrobe.

(ii) You can hang the expensive salwar suits on the right side of the closet on special hangers meant for them.

(iii) Shirts, T–shirts, short/long kurtas, mix and match salwar kameezes can be neatly folded and kept in the shelves if you don't have adequate space to hang them.

(iv) Last grouping will consist of blouses, petticoats, dupattas, undergarments, socks, handkerchiefs, purses, bags, fashion accessories and belts.

(v) Please refer the following suggested techniques of how to keep dupattas, undergarments and socks in your wardrobe.

(vi) For your jewellery, you can buy a jewellery box. Use cotton or tissue paper to protect them from moisture. A bangle holder or bangle box can hold your bangles in place. For your garlands/long chains, either you can hang them to a clip fixed on the door of your wardrobe or you can also store it in separate boxes. The shape should match the length of your neckwear. Don't forget to give it a lining. Now, if you don't have enough space in your wardrobe to accommodate your accessories, you can neatly store them in the utility drawer or even a shoe box will do. Never keep them with other important items like with pen, glasses, sunglasses, mobiles, etc. You will not only loose time in searching for a particular item but also the delicate accessories are affected due to abrasion with their relatively harsh neighbours.

3. **Use Trays**–You can use trays to keep your handkerchiefs, napkins, innerwear and other knick knacks. I personally recommend that you label the trays for better convenience. This way you will save a lot of time when you are getting ready for an occasion.

4. **Use Baskets**–You can use this to keep your children's socks collection, just hang the socks in pairs on the outer rim of

the basket, as you can see all the socks at one go, you can easily pick whatever you need. You can use the inside of the basket to keep undergarments.

5. **Rack for Tie and Dupatta**–Ask your carpenter to fix rods on the doors of your wardrobe. These would be the ideal place to hang your dupattas, husband's ties and socks. To prevent them from falling or to manage the colour arrangement you can always use clips or thick elastic bands meant for the hair.

6. To Keep Flowers Fresh

Usage of Preservatives

You can add various preservatives to the vase water to enhance the vase life. I have also explained the science behind it so that it becomes very easy for the laymen to understand it.

(i) Flower food (floral preservative), which one can buy from the local florist (this contains some chemicals).

(ii) Add a little bit of gin/vodka/sprite/seven Up and a teaspoon of sugar to the vase water.

(iii) Add one teaspoon of sugar, one teaspoon of bleach and two teaspoons of lemon juice / vinegar to a quart of lukewarm water. The sugar provides nutrition and will keep the flowers fresh, the bleach keeps the water free of bacteria and the lemon juice acidifies the wate:, decreasing its ph level. Bleach prevents the water from becoming stagnant and doesn't hurt the blooms.

(iv) You can add an aspirin in the vase water. Since it is acidic, it helps in combating the growth of bacteria.

(v) Add a copper coin. Since copper is a fungicidal it protects the water from yeasts and fungi.

Do not forget to change the water and renew your preservative mixture, every two days to keep your flowers fresh for a long time.

Proper Ways to Keep the Cut Flowers

(i) Place the cut flowers in a cool location, away from direct sunlight. Place the fresh flowers in the refrigerator for three to 12 hours. This cooling period will enable the flowers to absorb more water and stay fresher for longer time. Put them in the vegetable crisper for best results.

(ii) Put the cut flowers in a large vase of water as soon as possible.

(iii) If you are using a wide-necked vase, use scotch tape to form a grid of squares over the top, this will help hold the flowers in position.

(iv) If you have short or broken stems that you don't want to throw away, slip them into drinking straws cut to the required length.

(v) There is no need to keep the water level above the stems by more than six inches.

(vi) Re-trim the stems every few days. To prevent speedy wilting, cut the bottoms of the stems at a slight angle and remove all the leaves that will fall below the water level in the vase. This prevents bacterial growth which makes the water stink and shortens the life of the flowers.

(vii) For display, chop off dead and tightly closed buds from the stem as they will steal nutrients from the flower heads if you want to keep them healthy.

(viii) Always use lukewarm water for better absorption during your display. For tulips and hyacinths use cold water.

(ix) Don't overcrowd the flowers for your display.

(x) Some flowers like roses need special care. Usage of shower caps will keep roses fresh for two weeks! Just cover the flowers and keep them in the refrigerator loosely before you go to bed, remove the cap next day to enjoy your flowers. Their stems need to be trimmed under running cool water.

(xi) You can choose flowers that are long lasting like chrysanthemums, carnations and daisies.

(xii) If the flowers are in foam, or centerpiece, keep the foam well watered until the flowers die.

(xiii) Fleshy moist stemmed flowers like poppies usually don't draw well and need to be sealed with moisture to last longer. You can do this by dipping the tips into boiling water or singe the tip where you cut it as soon as you can with a lighter or match. Woody stems keep drawing well.

(xiv) Always cut flower stems with a sharp knife and not with a scissor. The later will bruise the stem and prevent proper water intake.

(xv) While cutting stems, always slice them at an angle of 45 degrees. This increases the area of stem that's exposed to water.

7. Take Care for Jewellery

The Do's

(i) Clean your gold ornaments periodically. An old soft toothbrush is an ideal tool to deal with the nooks and corners. Just soak them overnight in warm soapy water mixed with a spoonful of turmeric. You can use shampoo/mild detergent powder. Then wash it in plain cold water. You can use a strainer for extra precaution to prevent loss of smaller parts like ear studs and pushes.

(ii) Take your jewellery off before washing your hands and using cream as 'settings jewellery' can get clogged up with soap and hand cream.

(iii) Take them off (especially rings) when doing household chores like washing utensils, washing clothes, cooking and gardening. Heat emitted during cooking and hot water used in other household chores causes loosening of settings (pearl or precious stones in jewellery like rings, earrings, pendants, bangles, necklaces, etc.) where an adhesive has been used.

(iv) Always wear the jewellery after you have applied your cosmetics and sprays like deodorant spray, perfume, hairspray and nail polish remover. These products tend to discolour gold or make pearls turn yellow.

(v) Always protect your jewellery from sharp blows, scratching, chemicals, sunlight and heat/ cold. Ideally, store your jewellery in a soft lined box or pouch. Try to keep pieces apart, so that they don't rub together or tangle up. My personal advice is you can use a lot of soft paper napkins to segregate the different pieces.

(vi) Always try to keep your pearl ornaments between sheets of cotton. You can take a handful of cotton and beat them flat enough with your palm and wrap around your pearl wear. Cotton absorbs moisture from the air and thus prevents your pearl lose its lustre and brightness.

(vii) Whenever you are away from home, always carry a small velvety pouch where you can keep them safely after taking them off.

(viii) For beaded necklaces such as gemstone or pearls, store them flat, preferably in a silk pouch. If the string breaks, get it stringed by a professional jeweller.

The DON'Ts

(i) Never wear "fashion" jewellery on a regular basis, but keep them for special occasions.

(ii) Do not store pearls in plastic bags.

(iii) Don't wear too many chains at one time, they will tangle and rub off one another getting abraded.

(iv) Never go swimming in your jewellery, chlorine in swimming pools can cause damage to your jewellery.

8. **Matching Bedspread with Curtain**

   Suppose you have chosen a particular fabric for the curtain. You can also purchase to make a bedcover. If it is a double bed, you can stitch two pieces to make it a single looking one. With a little innovative idea you can also stitch some contrast colour borders to hide away the joints.

9. **Washing dustbin**–If you are comfortable wearing your rubber gloves, wear them or else wear a small plastic bag and tie around the palm of your right hand and clean the dustbin both inside and outside with the help of a scrubber and detergent. Then sun dry it and line it with a bin liner. You can also keep a small sachet of baking soda in the dustbin counter to absorb the repelling odour that normally accumulates in the kitchen over time.

10. **Washing Comb** – Wet all the combs. Then rub the bar soap along its length. Let them sit for a while. Then with the help of a toothbrush, clean all the teeth of a comb giving horizontal strokes at a time. Wash them in plain water.

11. **Soap Dish** – Follow the above procedure. You can place a piece of sponge, cut in the shape of a soap dish and keep the soap on top of it. This will keep the soap dish look clean for a long time. You can always clean the sponge once in a while.

12. **How to Keep Your Cooking Vessels Sparkling** – It is not possible to get this result with ordinary dish bar and scrubber.

    First step - is to buy polish paper/sand paper from any hardware store. Cut them into several small size pieces. Take a sharp knife and then rub it against the heavy burnt marks that have accumulated over time.

    Second Step – is to take one piece of the polish paper and moisten it with a little bit of oil.

    Final Step – is to scrub that part of the vessel that is not getting cleaned with normal soap and water, with this paper. Once you are done with the stains, wash it with normal soap and water.

13. **Cleaning Doormat** – First wash the doormats with ample plain water and then put it in the washing machine. If it is automatic, put it in the normal way. If it is semi automatic, put it in the third round. I suggest that you add some hydrogen peroxide/Dettol too as a disinfectant.

14. **Make Everyday Planning** – You should make a route map of your plans. First prioritize, then make a plan and then put them in actions. I have already suggested the ways and methods of doing household chores so that it saves your time and effort. Those who have domestic help can also use this book to guide them to get their things done to their satisfaction! Apart from cleaning vessels and mopping the floor you can also hire someone to perform odd jobs. Each day she can do a little whatever is assigned to her. You can divide the entire job and instruct her each day according to the work schedule. Time consuming tasks like peeling onion, ginger and garlic or scouring vessels to give a shiny appearance can be done once in a week/10 days/a fortnight, depending

upon your need. It can be done by you or your help while watching TV or listening to music so that the task doesn't appear boring.

Examples of a 'typical' **Things to do list/work to be done**

(A)

1. Take the kids to the doctor;
2. Buy medicines;
3. Peeling ginger and garlic;
4. Masterjee (local tailor who does odd jobs like mending work) for all the mending work needed to be done for your kids clothes as well as for the upholstery customisation of your home.

(B)

1. Attend the Open house of your kid;
2. Get your wash basins, mirrors and toilets cleaned by maid;
3. Go to Reliance Fresh for Grocery shopping;
4. Go to the cobbler for mending your son's school bag/shoes.

(C)

1. Go to Arcee (the shop from where you have purchased your electronics goods) to lodge a complaint for your washing machine;
2. Get one kg onion, ask maid to chop it and fry till brown. You can come home and make the paste and store them in your freezer :
3. Buy party items (decorative items, return gifts, etc.) for your kid's birthday
4. Order the cake.

(D)

1. Take mother-in law-to an orthopedic;

2. Get the two ceiling fans and two fixtures cleaned by the maid;
3. Order gas cylinder;
4. Sit with the kids to help them prepare for their exam.

And the list will go on and on. On these days don't you think it would be a blessing if you find a meal ready for you sitting in your freezer! All you have to do is thaw it, warm it and enjoy fresh homemade meal with your family.

15. **Do the Filing System for Household Official Matters –** Buy several plastic folders for your official household matters.
    (a) Electricity bills
    (b) Telephonebills
    (c) Mobilebills
    (d) Consumer durables like television, refrigerator, washing machine, microwave, air conditioner, etc.
    (i) Guarantee/warranty along with their manuals.
    (ii) Their bills.
    (e) House rental receipt and agreement copy (if rented house)
    (f) House EMI with relevant necessary documents (if you own the house).
    (g) Insurance policy documents. Mark one folder for one insurance policy, so if you have five policies you will need five folders.
    (h) Credit card related documents.
    (i) Bank related documents. (same as Insurance policy documents)
    (j) Coupons, discounts and facilities.
    (k) Medical (one folder for one member).
    (l) Reimbursement for fuel, etc.

(m) Children – birth certificate, passport size photographs, vaccination certificate, school reports, certificates and other accolades.

4
Uses of Baking Soda

(i) Baking soda can be very effective at removing stains and odour formed by :

- Acid spills or due to vomit/urine.
- Long usage of fabrics. As it is a natural cleaner, your older linens can be trusted to be whitened and brightened by its effects.
- Crayons.

(ii) Use a paste made of baking soda and water to wash the inside of your washing machine, refrigerator and microwave oven.

(iii) Try sprinkling baking soda :

- At the bottom of your dustbin to eliminate odours there.
- Inside your smelly shoes.

It helps to get rid of clogged drains.

Uses of Hydrogen Peroxide

You will be amazed to know that this chemical compound has numerous uses and applications in the domestic household as well. The various uses can be mainly attributed to its amazing oxidizing and bleaching properties. It is a natural disinfectant, antiseptic and sanitizer. It can be bought from the local drugstores. It comes in brown bottles that can filter out sunlight, as it breaks down quite quickly when exposed to light. Hydrogen peroxide is created in the atmosphere when ultraviolet rays from the sun hit oxygen in the presence of moisture. It is basically the same chemical make up as water but with an extra oxygen atom. Because of this it breaks down quickly and harmlessly into oxygen and water.

How to Use Hydrogen Peroxide

Use the three per cent undiluted solution in a spray bottle and spray it on the surface to be cleaned. Allow it to stand for several minutes and then wipe it off. Surfaces that can be cleaned with hydrogen peroxide are countertops, glass, sinks, mirror, windows, shower doors, bathtubs, toilets, walls, etc.

Versatile Uses

1. You can soak fingernails and toenails in it to remove stains.
2. You can use it to prevent wax buildup in the ears. Tilt your head to expose the ear to be treated. Using an eye dropper, you should put two-three drops into the ear and allow it to settle for a several minutes, let it stay for a few seconds, until it stops fizzing completely. The head has to be tilted sideways before putting hydrogen peroxide in ear. After a few seconds, the head is tilted in the opposite direction to drain out the hydrogen peroxide. Hydrogen peroxide causes an effervescence reaction, which helps to bring out the trapped debris and wax from the ear. However, it should be kept in mind that only three percent hydrogen peroxide is used for ear wax removal and external ear infection treatment. With a syringe filled with warm water, carefully flush the ear out. Then dry your ear using a soft dry cloth.
   (a) **Note:** If the eardrum is perforated, one should never use hydrogen peroxide for ear wax removal.
3. You can also soak the following things in it to disinfect them :
   - Tooth brushes, Toilet brushes, Dish scrubbers, Kitchen clothes, Sponges, Dental retainers, Loofahs and other bath items.

- Items used by any sick family members; bedpans, thermometers, etc.
- Items needed for the new born and infants like cotton nappies, wash cloth, oil cloth, baby potty chair, etc.

4. Remove blood stains on clothes.

   Note: This is bleach and it can leave bleached spots on darker colours causing fading. If you have any doubt, it is always advisable to test a swatch of the fabric with hydrogen peroxide before using.

5. To clean fruits and vegetables of pesticide and herbicide residues, pour in salt and ¼ cup of hydrogen peroxide into a container full of water. Wash with cold water and drain after soaking them. This process also kills harmful bacteria like E. Coli. Alternatively, you can use a 50/50 mixture of hydrogen peroxide and water to spray the fruits and vegetables. Don't worry about flavour because hydrogen peroxide does not affect the food's taste and texture.
6. One major use by the gardeners is Spanish water. It is basically just a weak hydrogen peroxide solution and is used to treat root rot and to encourage root development.
7. Mix an ounce of hydrogen peroxide with a cup of water, which can then be used as a "green" pest controller as well as a rich source of oxygen for your plants. Just spray whenever and wherever necessary.
8. If you have an aquarium, you can use hydrogen peroxide to control fungi present in fishes and their eggs. It has been classified safe for fish use by the Food and Drug Administration (FDA).

Uses of Shampoo

1. For a stuck zipper, put a drop of shampoo on a Q-tip and dab it onto the zipper. This will help the zipper to slide easily. You can also rub a wax candle along the length of the zip.

2. You can bring back life into your expensive leather shoes and purses by buffing your shoes with a few drops of shampoo on a piece of clean cloth.
3. I personally opine that you can reduce your expenses by washing your expensive linens and silks (Non-Zari ones) with shampoo instead of giving them to the laundry.
4. Dip a towel in a solution of shampoo and water. Wring it and use it to clean your indoor plants.
5. It is indispensable cleanser in cleaning any spill on your carpet and upholstery items. Just blot it with a wet towel.
6. A few drops of shampoo rubbed onto the inside surface of a swimming mask will prevent the mask from fogging up. Then rinse it off.
7. If you are a proud car owner, use shampoo for a great clean. It can be mixed with baking soda to clean chrome on vehicles.
8. Apply a few drops of it to loosen stuck nuts, bolts and hinges.

Uses of Toothpaste

1. You can apply a bit of the paste (Fluoride based) on to your silver ornaments and silverware/diamond and leave overnight. Gently scrub it with a wet toothbrush with soft bristles and then wipe clean with a soft cloth in the morning.
2. To clean the lens of your goggles.
3. To clean keys of piano/synthesizer/any other musical instruments.
4. To remove crayon marks made by the kids on your walls.
5. To remove all traces of strong and pungent odour like garlic, fish and onion from your hands and fingertips.
6. To remove tough stains from clothing by applying it directly to the stain and rubbing briskly until the spot is gone. Then wash in the usual way.

Note: Whitening toothpaste can bleach the colour fabric. Therefore be careful while using it.

7. Since our teeth and fingernails are made of enamel, to get cleaner, shinier, and stronger nails, simply scrub the underneath and tops of fingernails with a toothbrush and toothpaste. This is really effective to clean yellow stains on the nails.
8. **Numerous medicinal applications** – It stops itching and reduce the swelling to a significant extent when applied to the affected area caused by a bug bite or insect sting. It dries and heals the wound faster when applied to sores or blisters. It provides immediate temporary cooling relief to minor burns.

   Note: It should not be applied on an open wound.
9. To remove the burned crust in the iron plate which develops overtime. The silica in toothpaste gently grinds away this rusty-looking crust.

Uses of White Vinegar

1. Add a few tablespoons to the water when boiling eggs. If any shells crack, the whites won't leak out.
2. Perk your wilted leafy veggies / lettuce / spinach by soaking them in cold water with a little vinegar.
3. To eliminate the odour of raw onions from your hands.
4. While cooking vegetables like cabbage, broccoli, cauliflower, turnip or radish, adding a little vinegar to the water will reduce the flatulence they can induce.
5. Spray vinegar to pre-treat the stains caused by deodorants, mustard sauce, tomato sauce or ketchup.
6. To loosen chewing gum stuck to car upholstery, rugs, and carpet.
7. Use three-to-one vinegar-water mixture to wipe down your car windows and windshield to keep them frost-free during winter.

8. Wipe your pet's itchy ears with undiluted vinegar to prevent them from scratching their ears.

Uses of Lemon and Lemon Rind

Lemon juice is about five to six percent citric acid and has a pH level two-three. Due to this property, it gently breaks down rust and mineral stains, without making the surface dull.

1. Sprinkle some salt (for abrasion) on a lemon half and rub on the greasy areas like gas top, greasy pans, kitchen counters, etc. Let it sit for a while. Then clean those areas with a little lukewarm water, plastic scrubber and dish bar.
   Note: Never use it on marble surface.
2. Fill the kettle with water. Put a few slices of lemon peel and bring to a boil. Turn off heat and let sit for an hour. Strain and wash in the normal way. You will be delighted to find the mineral deposit that builds up over time in your tea kettle vanishing. To remove coffee stains, use lemon rinds, salt and ice. Follow the same procedure.
3. Add lemon rinds to a microwave-safe bowl half filled with water. Cook on high for five minutes, allowing the water to boil and the steam to condense on the walls and tops of the oven. Carefully remove the hot bowl and wipe away the mess with a towel.
   Note: Use an oven mitt.
4. Rub a squeezed lemon half dipped in salt or baking powder to brighten copper cookware, as well as brass, chrome or stainless steel. The citric acid in it is effective enough to remove mineral deposits on chrome faucets. Rinse and lightly buff with a soft cloth to make it shine.
5. Refresh cutting boards by rubbing it with a halved lemon. It also removes the black stains gathered over time.
6. Put some lemon rind in your brown sugar to keep it moist and easy to use.

7. **Make zest**–Zest is grated peel. It is easier to grate the zest from the lemon before juicing them. You can grate it with a box grater. To dry zest, spread it on a towel and leave out until dried, then store in a jar. You can freeze in zip lock bag also.

   Note: This zest is used in the recipe of lemon souffle. Orange/ lemon zest can be added in the batter used to make fruit loafs/cakes. It lends a unique enhanced flavor to the dish. This can be used for marination of meat/chicken also. In case you don't have any flavoured essence handy at home, try using zest of any kind. I bet you will be amazed by the result.
8. Lemon/orange/grapefruit peel can be candied too. It is yummy! They can be eaten plain, dipped in melted chocolate (chocolate fondue), used in cake, assorted cookie and bread recipes.
9. **Beauty applications** – It helps in lightening age spots if lightly rubbed on the face. Use a half lemon sprinkled with baking soda on elbows to lighten the complexion. Rinse and dry. Make a great body scrub by mixing half a cup of sugar with finely chopped lemon peel and enough olive oil to make a paste. Apply all over your body and rinse to get a refreshing feel.

Uses of the Blow Dryer

1. You can dry your nail polish.
2. Your children have accidentally dropped a little water on their clothes. You are running short of time to fish out another set of clothes, take the help of dryer to dry the wet spill. If it is some other liquid other than water like milk, juice or chocolate, first treat that particular area as follows: Take a damp hand towel / wet tissue and put some Old Spice / liquid soap onto it. Rub the affected area with this. Then wipe it off with another fresh wet towel /wet tissue. Finally dry it with the dryer as usual.

Note: It would require lesser time to actually do it than reading this tip.

3. To dry up painting either stain glass, or the block print on a cushion /canvas.
4. Blast some hot air onto the lid to thaw the frost in case you face some difficulty while opening the lid of a container.

Uses of Tooth Brush

1. To fluff Barbie doll's hair/Santa's beard.
2. To clean up the inside and out, neck of the glass/glass bottles/ jars/sipper cups.
3. To add texture to clay models in your art project.
4. It cleans the bottom of sliding door casement area and it gets into the nooks and crannies very well. Clean the dirt and buildup with the toothbrush dry, then take a wet sponge with liquid cleaner and then dry well with a paper towel.
5. To clean around the sinks, faucets and hinges of the toilet seats.
6. To clean the hardened crumbs on the wire areas and the sides of the toaster.
7. To clean dog shoes soles.
8. To clean between the lines of forks while washing cutlery and box grater or the blades of a food processor.
9. To scrub the rocks in your aquarium.
10. It is equally effective in dusting any sophisticated electronics products.
11. It also appears to be functional in scrubbing that part of the tea or coffee pot where the water comes out.
12. To scrub bird's cage. Don't forget to label it as 'birds' to ensure hygiene.
13. It can be used for spot cleaning garments. It is useful in removing stains off white fabric which also has other colours

on it. Dip the toothbrush into the bleach and carefully remove the stain without bleaching the surrounding coloured areas.

14. Clean your fingernails after gardening.
15. To clean the radio knobs, parking brake, gear shift/air vents inside the car.
16. To clean window screens, tile grout, corners on window sills, French doors, etc.

Uses of Freezer Bags

1. Please refer to my earlier techniques of cleaning gold and silver jewelry. Use freezer bags to ease out your job in handling so many items.
2. It's always inconvenient for many people to use the juicer or food processor when it comes for making juice. The best option I have discovered is throw good amount of any citrus fruits/grapes/pomegranate/even lauki and give it two turns in the mixer/blender. Now pour everything inside a bag and give it a good wring to extract juice in a tumbler.
3. You can also put small things like under garment, socks, hair bands, etc., inside the bag and wash it in the machine in the usual way.
4. It is so effective in storing your child's play items. e.g., Lego pieces, Carrom dices, puzzle pieces.
5. Use it to store parts of your food processor, mobile accessories, etc.

5

How to De-clutter Your Home

If you are looking to create more space in your home, the best option is to de-clutter it. When you are surrounded by mess and disorganisation, you feel more mentally cluttered, less decisive, slightly anxious, and confused. I personally feel relaxed and get absolute peace of mind when I see any house including my house totally clean, organised, and clutter free. Advantages of a clean and organised home are:

1. Saves time as well as money in everyday household activity by reducing the chances of double buying.
2. Instills peace and harmony in your life.
3. You are enveloped by positive energy.

This book is.... meant for the following people:

1. Those who always tell themselves and others that they have no time, as excuse to delay organising their apartment.
2. Those who are tired of getting rid of the clutter in your home.
3. Those who hesitate bringing their friends over to their place.

Phase 1

To create more storage space, first get rid of clothes, books, utensils, accessories that are no longer used by the family. First take six separate sacks or boxes and label them with the six catagories:

1. **Trash/garbage** – Items that are not re-usable/cannot be repaired/is too old to be donated.
2. **Give Away/Charity** – Be generous. First think about your immediate surroundings. Those serving in the same

community like domestic help, watchmen, iron man, driver, the municipal cleaner, even your regular milkman, grocery or vegetable vendor. You can always pass on the old clothes, shoes, accessories to them. For the rest of the items, you can think about the nearby orphanages /NGO run centres where your contributions would really make a significant impact. It can range from uncared plants to baby shoes, kids toys, clothes to magazines, extra old vessels which you do not use anymore. Unused but still edible bottles of jam, jelly or pickles . . . unused medicines (check for the expiry dates.)

3. **Sale**

(a) Raddiwala for old newspaper, bottles, tin cans, etc.

(b) **Garage sale** – Though this is a western concept, I personally do not like the idea to be applied in a developing country like India. But if you want to reap any financial gain of selling your unused but expensive stuff, you can think about the garage sale.

4. **Storage** – Put items in here that you cannot part with but do not need on a regular basis like modak maker, icing funnel, steamer, etc. Make an inventory of the items as you box them. Group similar items together. One good way to clean out wardrobe is to store out of season clothing, e.g. During summer, you can keep away your winter garments, silks, etc. carefully inside the Divan/a steel or aluminium Trunk /Suitcase or air trolley. Similarly, during winter you can do away with sleeveless, short kurtis and the like, cotton clothes, etc., Don't forget to push a few naphthalene balls. In case you are averse to chemicals, you can try sachets containing whole red dried chillies and Onion seeds.

5. **Regular** – This should be your smallest category. These are items that need to be out on a regular basis. Organise according to my suggestions in the book.

6. **Mending** – This can include torn saree or kid's clothes which needs stitching, electronic items which needs to be repaired, or kitchen vessels or utility items which probably needs to be re-fitted with some screws.

Phase 2

After getting rid of all the unwanted things out of one's home, the need of the hour is to organise the remaining things. Make an effort in going through your existing storage spaces and also the potential vacant places. If needed, put up some extra shelves to fit in clothes and other items. If your closet is overstuffed, you can add some extra rods. If you have a small kitchen, try reorganising and utilize your wall space fully. You can install hooks or a hook grid to hang several pans, lids, kadais, etc.

Phase 3

Give each item a home and definitely try to remember their homes very well. Otherwise you can also write their names and homes in a diary and keep it above the fridge. The general tendency is to dump everything on the top of the nearest flat surfaces like top of the dining table, centre table, fridge, side table or the first drawer in sight. Once everything gets accumulated, it really looks like trash bin. It then not only becomes tiring to clean but to look at it as well. Now those of you who are reading this book don't wait for the book to finish. Gear up Right Now.

First step

Choose any one corner/one particular place you want to de clutter. It might be your table top or the lower shelf of your wardrobe. Throw everything from that surface into a cardboard box or bag.

Second step

Try to give instead of finding homes for each item in the bag.

Some Suggestions

1. Buy some attractive boxes of different colours or shapes to store all your loose items. Group like items together into boxes, so that they will be easy to find when needed. You don't have to waste your time in searching for it. List of examples can be any sorts of bills, receipts, credit card statement, gum, stapler, cellotape, pictures, wires, blank CDs, loose magazine cut-outs, pens, craft paper, chart paper, ribbons. Stationary items can go very well in one of the boxes. Always label them and write its home in your diary.
2. You can put chart paper, glue, ribbons, pictures, old calendars, craft papers, etc. in big shopper (large jute bag) and keep it away. Put a label as 'school project'. If you do not have a proper closet to accommodate this, at least you can cover it with a newspaper or old cloth and keep it neatly under the master bed. Don't forget to write this in your diary.
3. You can buy some coloufui plastic folders to store magazine/ newspaper cut outs and write 'personal'.
4. All sorts of medicines and medicine bottles should be scrutinised to check their expiry date and properly kept inside a closet away from the reach of children and sunlight.
5. Find small boxes for your utility drawer. Get a box for every small item that you keep in your drawer or closet. For example, batteries, stamps, elastic bands, random pens, scissors, notepads, etc.

Phase 4

Stick to the previous steps religiously. Make it a point not to place anything and everything on the open surface. Work upon your old habits. Try giving rewards to your kids to inculcate this habit in them at a very early age.

Common Habits by People

Lay the shirt/jacket/suit/blazer at the back of a chair when they come home. Hang the trouser on the hook at the back of the door. All the other things lying scattered on the floor. Keeping stationeries/accessories on the dining table. Make it part of your daily ritual not to repeat whatever you have done before. It would take some time, but believe me at the end you will be really happy to see your beautiful home.

First Step

Do not procrastinate, however small your task may be. When you're done with something, put it away immediately.

Examples :

1. When you finish a school project, put everything away. Ask your children to follow this principle. They will respect you for this when they grow up.
2. Clothes are an integral part of one's lifestyle. Be very particular about it. My principle is they should be worn upon one's body /neatly folded in the closet/in the laundry basket/on the clothes line to dry. During summer most of the people tend to keep it outside the closet to let the sweat dry up. I advise you to let it dry on the cloths line or inside a special closet meant for the sweat clothes. By implementing small gestures in your daily life, you can really improve the ambience in your "Home Sweet Home". My sole expectation from all the readers of my book is to be proactive in the humble process of de-cluttering.

Second Step

Start Acting SMART and HUMBLE

I advise you to go through the wardrobe of your entire family. If you find any saree which is unsuitable to wear in the metros, think whether you can give it to someone in your hometown/ village. You can also think of other clothing which you have not worn in more than two years. You can renovate them with your ideas like making cushion covers out of old tissue or silk kameez. You can make a table spread or a throw away for your sofa out of your old but bright coloured dupattas, if you do not want to wear them simply because it is out of fashion. You can modify it and give it to your maid. Children's clothes, shoes, toys, etc. can be donated to maids or drivers children.

DVDs you'll never watch again, books you'll never read again, kitchen stuff you haven't used for more than a year, because you have got some new fancy items. Do not think twice about its cost, etc. just give it to them who can't afford or donate them to an old home / orphanage centre.

Experts Tip – You can write out on your diary, all the sections of your home that need a makeover. After that make each one a mini-project, which you can tackle every week/weekend. This way, the cleaning tasks will appear manageable and will not take all day.

6
How to Ensure Safe Handling of Foods

At the Frozen Sections in the Market

1. **Shop for cold food** (perishable foods – Such as meats, fish, poultry, frozen processed foods, vegetables, peas and dairy products) last. Bacteria thrive at room temperature. After you shop, immediately get your groceries home and into the refrigerator fast.
2. **Avoid 'grocery cart cross-contamination'** which can occur when juices from raw meat, fish or poultry come into contact with other foods, utensils or surfaces. **Wrap perishables in plastic** before placing them in your shopping basket or trolley so they won't drip on other items.

At Home

3. **Follow the 'First in, First Out' rule of thumb.** Organise your refrigerator and freezer with the older foods in front or on the top so they will be used first. Zip lock plastic bags are a convenient choice because you can write the date and content right on the bag. Same principle to be followed while keeping fruits and vegetables in the vegetable basket of the refrigerator.
4. **Prevent Oxidation to retain the flavour and nutrients.** Oxygen is a major cause of food spoilage and vitamin loss. When using plastic wrap, bags or containers to store perishables, squeeze the air out and seal lids tight. Store food

in small, shallow (preferably less than two inches deep) containers with lids. This will conserve space and help to prevent freezer burn.

5. **Keep your kitchen fresh and clean.** Before handling, cooking and serving food, wash your hands with hot, soapy water and make sure that all cooking utensils, equipment and surfaces are clean. Try to keep sponges, dishrags and dishcloths fresh too.

Food Storage Safety Tips for the Refrigerator and Freezer

- **Check your temperature.** Food safety experts at the U.S. Food and Drug Administration recommend keeping refrigerators at or below 40 degrees Fahrenheit (5°C) and freezers at or below zero degrees Fahrenheit (minus 18°C). Allowing your fridge or freezer to get too warm can decrease foods' shelf life and increase the growth of unhealthy bacteria.
- **Fruits and vegetables: Store first, wash later.** In most cases, it is better to wash them just before eating.
- **Two-hour max.** Foods should be contained and stored in a refrigerator or freezer within two hours after cooking.
- **Freezing** does not eliminate bacteria or parasites. Although it does prevent the growth of microbes, freezing won't eliminate those that already exist in your food.
- **Keep cool during a power cut.** If the refrigerator power goes out, foods should keep for one - two days depending on the contents. Fuller refrigerators generally preserve foods longer than empty ones. Be sure to keep the refrigerator door(s) closed as much as possible until power is restored.
- **Plan ahead.** Make a point of using stored foods before opening or purchasing more and try to note down the expiry dates of all you have bought in your kitchen diary.

- **When in doubt, throw it out.** If you're not sure whether a food item has gone bad, remember that smelling or tasting the food is not a good indicator of safety. That's because most harmful bacteria can't be seen, smelled or tasted.
- Tired of the same **old leftovers**? (Refer to my Tips) on **"Best out of waste"**.

Food Specific Storage Tips

Learn how to use your refrigerator more efficiently to keep your vegetables at the peak of their flavour. Factors to consider in storing vegetables include:

- What's the optimal temperature?
- How much humidity is best?
- Which vegetables absorb or release odours?
- Which vegetables absorb or release ethylene?

Get to Know your Fefrigerator

The temperature in your refrigerator should be 34°C 40°F (1°–4°C). Pathogenic (disease-carrying) bacteria thrive above 40°F. Below 40°F, spoilage bacteria can still grow on foods - affecting their taste and smell – but they're not generally harmful. If the temperature is too low, vegetables can freeze.

Most refrigerators have special compartments or "crisper drawers" to store fruits and vegetables, often with slide mechanisms to control the humidity in the drawer. A closed setting keeps moist air in – good for vegetables that like high humidity such as leafy greens, cucumbers, root vegetables, celery, leeks, summer squash, and peppers. With more than one crisper drawer, you can group vegetables by their temperature and humidity needs. Crisper drawers are most effective when they're at least two-thirds full.

Freezing – If freezing is properly done, you can preserve the colour, texture, flavor and also the nutritional value of the vegetables. Thus, we can consume seasonal vegetables and even fruits like mangoes (their pulps) throughout the year.

Guidelines to be Followed While Freezing Vegetables

1. Though freezing slows down the activity of the enzymes responsible for unpleasant odours, the loss of colour and nutrients in vegetables, it does not neutralise the effect of the enzymes completely. To make the freezing process more effective, blanch before freezing. Only vegetables with high acid content, such as tomatoes, do not need to be blanched prior to freezing.
2. Only freeze vegetables that are fresh and have reached peak ripeness.
3. Never overload the freezer with a large quantity of food to be frozen at one time.
4. To freeze vegetables as quickly as possible, maintain a constant temperature of 0°F or less. At this temperature, vegetables will keep for about a year.
5. **Cold Storage Chart**

The following selections are from the U.S. Department of Agriculture and the U.S. Food and Drug Administration's Cold Storage Chart. As the USDA and FDA note, the specified time limits on refrigerated foods will ensure they don't spoil and become unsafe to eat. Frozen foods can be stored indefinitely, but the taste and texture of the food may change after the time limits listed below. The complete chart is available at www.foodsafety.gov/~fsg/f01chart.html.

Product	Refrigerator (40°F)	Freezer (0°F)
Eggs		
Fresh, in shell	3 to 5 weeks	Don't freeze
Hard cooked	1 week	Don't freeze well
Soup and Stews		
Vegetable or meat added	3 to 4 days	2 to 3 months
Meat Left Overs		
Cooked meat and meat casseroles	3 to 4 days	2 to 3 months
Gravy and meat broth	1 to 2 days	2 to 3 months
Fresh Poultry		
Chicken or turkey, whole	1 to 2 days	1 year
Chicken or turkey, pieces	1 to 2 days	9 months
Cooked Poultry		
Fried chicken	3 to 4 days	4 months
Pieces, plain	3 to 4 days	4 months
Chicken nuggets, patties	1 to 2 days	1 to 3 months
Pizza		
Pizza	3 to 4 days	1 to 2 months
Stuffing		
Stuffing-cooked	3 to 4 days	1 month
Beverages, Fruit		
Juices in cartons, fruit drinks, punch	3 weeks unopened 7 to 10 days opened	8 to 12 months
Dairy		
Butter	1 to 3 months	6 to 9 months
Cheese, Hard (such as Cheddar, Swiss)	6 months, unopened 3 to 4 weeks, opened	6 months
Cheese, Soft (such as Brie, Bell Pease)	1 week	6 months
Paneer	1 week	Doesn't freeze well
Cream Cheese	2 weeks	Doesn't freeze well
Margarine	4 to 5 months	12 months
Milk	7 days	3 months

Sour cream	7 to 21 day	Doesn't freeze
Yogurt	7 to 14 days	1 to 2 months
Fish		
Lean fish (cod, flounder, haddock, sole, etc.)	1 to 2 days	6 months
Fatty fish (bluefish, mackerel, salmon, etc.)	1 to 2 days	2 to 3 months
Cooked fish	3 to 4 days	4 to 6 months
Smoked fish	14 days or date on vacuum package	2 months in vacuum package
Shrimp, scallops, crayfish, squid, shucked clams, mussels and oysters	1 to 2 days	3 to 6 months
Live clams, mussels, crab, lobster and oysters	2 to 3 days	2 to 3 months
Cooked shellfish	3 to 4 days	3 months

7

Microwave Cooking: The Basics

- Arrange evenly sized pieces of food in a circle for more even cooking. If food happens to be different sizes, place thicker pieces toward the outer edges and smaller pieces toward the centre.
- While cooking food that have a skin or some other type of shell or coating, pierce the outer layer. This will prevent food from exploding due to steam that can build up from the insides like eggs and potatoes. So either prick them or slit them.
- Make sure your container is labeled for microwave use.
- Using containers that are round or oval in shape can help to heat food more evenly. With square or rectangular shaped containers, the corners tend to receive more energy, which can cause food to overcook in these areas.
- Many recipes and packaging labels provide a cooking time that is expressed as a range (e.g., cook three-five min. on High) rather than an exact time period. To avoid overcooking, it's a good idea to check the food at the lower end of the suggested range (in this case, three minutes). You can always decide to cook it longer.
- Always remember to use an oven mitt (gloves) while taking out the dish.
- Always transfer partially cooked/defrosted food directly from the microwave to your oven, stove or grill. Do not keep thawed foods in storage for later use.

- Always remember to cover your food (to prevent spillage) with a perforated lid (to allow steam to escape) in the microwave.
- After cooking, lift container lids and wraps carefully, facing away from you, so that hot steam is released safely. Be careful not to burn yourself.
- Salt on the surface of food tends to attract microwaves, which can dry out the outer layer. If salt is desired, sprinkle it on the food after removal from the microwave.
- To clean the inside of your microwave oven, refer to the previous sections.

Food Specific Microwave Cooking Tips

- Thaw frozen juices by heating in a microwavable container for approximately 30 seconds.
- Keep morning coffee, tea or hot chocolate fresh by covering leftovers with plastic wrap and placing in the fridge. Reheat one mug at a time for one-two minutes on high power. Prior to microwaving, peel and loosen plastic wrap to allow steam to escape. You can also warm your infant or kid's milk bottle.
- Soften chilled butter by reducing power to 50 per cent and heating for approximately 40 seconds.
- When heating cream or sour cream, lower the power to 50-75 per cent to help avoid curdling.
- Soften hard-packed brown sugar by placing in a microwavable container with a slice of apple or a slice of fresh bread and cover loosely with plastic wrap. Heat on high for approximately 30 seconds.
- Make breadcrumbs by cutting bread slices into cubes and microwaving on high until hard.
- To renew hardened honey, microwave for approximately one minute.

- Melt chocolate squares by heating at full power for approximately 45 seconds per ounce of chocolate. You can also refer the double boiling technique.
- Soften rock-hard ice cream by heating at 30 per cent power for approximately 20 seconds.
- To dry lemon and orange peel, place grated rind in small microwavable container and heat on high power for approximately 30 to 60 seconds.
- Microwave lemons and other citrus fruits for approximately 20 seconds to help get more juice when squeezed.
- To plump dried raisins and other dried fruits, sprinkle water. Cover loosely with plastic wrap and heat on high approximately 30 seconds.
- Dry herbs/Roast nuts in the microwave by spreading into a single layer between paper towels and heating at full power for approximately two-three minutes.
- To help maximize flavour, try adding herbs after food has been cooked or heated in the microwave.
- Crisp stale chips, cookies or crackers by microwaving them at full power for approximately 10 seconds.
- Blanch nuts by placing them in boiling water and heating on high up to one minute. Remove skins by rubbing between paper towels.
- Veggies can be steamed with no added fat by placing them in a microwavable container with one to two tablespoons of water and cover loosely with plastic wrap. Cook on high until soft.
- Make great corn on the cob by rinsing ears in cold water with the husks on. Heat in the microwave on high for up to six minutes for two ears and up to eight minutes for four.

8

Top Eight Plastic Essentials

1. **Plastic Cutting Boards** – provide non-porous surfaces for food preparation that make them less likely to harbor bacteria. Food experts recommend maintaining at least two separate cutting boards – one for raw meats, fish and poultry and another for fruits and vegetables. Be sure to clean them thoroughly after each use.
2. **'Grown Up' Plastic Containers** – of varying shapes and sizes can help provide safe, convenient storage for leftovers and allows for storage in serving sizes appropriate for lunches or snacks on the run.
3. **Plastic Wrap and Sealable Bags** – Seal in freshness, flavour and nutrients and can help heat food evenly and prevent splatter. Sealable bags can provide quick, safe storage of sandwiches and snacks on the go. Large sealable bags can be used to safely marinate meat, fish and poultry. Just flip over the bag to redistribute marinade.
4. **Colander** – is ideal for draining pasta, noodles, rinsing vegetables like spinach, any leafy vegetables and fruits like grapes and more. Keep it near the sink for easy access.
5. **Cooking Utensils** – Many plastic spoons, spatulas and other cooking utensils are resistant to high heats and are essential to prevent scratching the surface of nonstick pots and pans.
6. **Drawer, Organisers and Knife Sleeves** – These help in organizing cutlery, etc. and prevent the hazards of fumbling around among sharp objects. For added protection of good knives and your hands, store knives in a plastic knife sleeve.

You can also try making a homemade one by making use of a cutout sleeve of a worn/faded shirt.

7. **Plastic Mixing Bowls** – are great for salad mixing, preparing batter for fried foods, marinating veg/non-veg items and Making popcorn and the list follows.
8. **Microwave Splatter Shield** – To avoid greasy and messy splatter in the microwave.

9

Best Out of Waste

Whatever my suggestions are, they are not going to work if you have people who are difficult to deal with. It is indeed a Herculean task to keep a home by following my suggestions if some family members are sadistic/critical/conventional/not open to new ideas.

1. **Dalpuri Out of Dal** – Heat some oil, put some cumin seeds. When they begin to splutter, add some chopped onion, and green chillies. Sauté them for two - three minutes. Then add the leftover dal. Put it on medium heat, stir it continuously. When it has turned into a dry consistency, put the flame off. Allow to cool. Then make some stuffed parathas with it by applying a bit of oil or ghee on both sides. Serve with curd/raita/pickle/ketchup and salad of your choice.
2. **Stuffed Paratha Out of Leftover Vegetables** – Repeat the above procedure. You can add chopped coriander leaves, chat masala / dried Amchur powder to the stuffing as optional. If you like the taste of hing, you can add a pinch to the heated oil before adding the vegetables.
3. **Thick Chicken soup out of Left over Chicken Roast** – Dissolve one cube of Maggi chicken stock cube in enough water and make a thick stock. You can add some cornflour or leftover mashed potatoes to thicken it further. Add shredded chicken from the roast. Finish it up with seasonings of your choice like salt, pepper, oregano, rosemary, etc. You can also add diced fresh vegetables like carrots, beans, mushroom and broccoli to get steaming hot vegetable soup.
4. **Biriyani Out of Leftover Chicken or Mutton** – Soak the

basmati rice for half an hour. Heat the oil in a pressure cooker. Add whole spices (cinnamon stick, green cardamom and bay leaves) and sliced onions. Sauté for a while till brown. Drain water from the rice and add to the masalas. Mix the meat and add double the amount of water. Put the flame high and put it off just before the first whistle. You can also add roasted potatoes and garnish with boiled eggs.

5. **Mixed Noodles/fried rice Out of Leftover salad and dry non–veg items–** Boil and drain the noodles and toss it with chopped veggies (except cucumber) and meat. Since the salad already contains enough of seasoning, you simply don't need to add anything. I repeat that the choice will depend upon your preferences as everything is optional.
6. **Chinese Idli** – Heat some oil in a wok. Add chopped garlic, onion, capsicum and green chillies. Fry for a while. Then add the leftover idlies (by cutting into small bite size pieces). Add seasoning and sauce of your choice. Mix well and serve hot.
7. **Vegatable Tikki Chops** – If you have some veggies other than potatoes, add some mashed potatoes. Put some chat masala and seasoning of your choice. Give some desired shape. Roll it over some Rawa. Shallow fry and serve with ketchup and onion wedges.
8. **Chatpata Fried Rice** – Sauté some onion and slited green chillies, add green peas, chopped carrots, bit of sprouts, sweet corn (optional). Then finally put leftover rice. Add some seasoning. Put some roasted groundnut. Mix well and serve hot with curd / pickle. **Variation** - Put mustard seeds, curry leaves, a dash of hing, bit of grated coconut/juice of half a lemon to give the South Indian flavour. Saute some onion, chopped bell pepper, a few cloves of garlic and then put rice. Then add a dash of ajinomoto to give a Chinese flavour.

9. **Rice Chilla** – Take a cup of cooked rice. Mash it with the back of a ladle. Mix a cup of whole wheat flour. You can also add half a portion of gram flour. Then add chopped spring onion greens, green chillies, salt as per taste and warm water to make soft dough. Roll out into chappatis and cook on a tawa with little oil on both sides.
10. **Chapati Poha** – Dry roast the leftover chapattis in a tawa. Cut them into bits of pieces. Heat some oil in a kadai. Put some mustard and cumin seeds, dry red chillies, hing (optional). When the seeds start to splutter, put some chopped onions and green chillies, fry for a while. Then add the chapati pieces. Add salt and mix well. Garnish with chopped coriander leaves and lemon wedges and serve. **Variation** – Add a little bit of dahi, sweet tamarind chutney. Top it up with some farsan of your choice and roasted masala powder. Serve this homemade chaat in a jiffy.
11. **Chapati Pakora** – Make a batter of dropping consistency with gram flour, salt, a pinch of baking soda and water. Dip the chapati pieces and deep fry them. Serve hot with ketchup. You can also dip them in egg batter and deep fry.
12. **Sweet poha** – Crumble all the various types of sweets which boast your refrigerator shelf. Heat some oil in a kadai. Add some grated coconut and fry for a while. Then add freshly washed and drained poha, crumbled sweets, small cardamom (optional) and mix well. Top it up with some chopped dry fruits of your choice (optional). Serve this tasty sweet poha to your loved ones.
13. **Triffle Pudding out of Assorted Cakes and a Few Fruits** - First crumble all the cakes and cookies you have in a large bowl. Whip up two eggs with some butter. Fold the crumbled mixture into it gently. Add chopped fruits if you want to. Then grease a mould and place the mixture onto it. Steam it for about half an hour. Serve with fresh cream / custard / vanilla ice cream.

14. **Stuffed Pancakes** – Make a batter with maida and butter milk/eggs and milk, with a little amount of sugar and a pinch of baking soda. You can make stuffed pancakes with the above mentioned crumbled mixture in (no. 12)
15. **Papad Samosa** – Make a filling as in point 2. and 3. Divide the papad into two halves. Take one half and give the shape of a samosa and stuff it with this filling. Give a neat fold with your wet fingers. Deep fry and serve.
16. **Chicken/Vegetable Wrap** – Heat a little bit of oil. Add leftover vegetables (chopped)/leftover Chole/rajma or chicken/ mutton (shredded). Fry for a while till it is dry. Put seasoning and sauce of your choice. Add juliennes of onion, capsicum, and chopped green chilies, lettuce (optional). Use this as a filling for your wrap by placing it in your regular tawa chapatti/you can use this as a filling for your normal sandwich by placing it between two slices of bread on top of lettuce and a bed of corns. You can also use dinner roll.

    Note: Here we are only going to make use of dry leftover dish.
17. **Variety in non-Veg Curry**

(a) Take a kadai, put the Chicken / mutton gravy into it. Put the heat on. Add juliennes of onion, capsicum, ginger and green chilies (slitted), when it starts to boil, put a small bundle (preferably in muslin) containing a few kafir lime leaves, lemon rind and a few strings of lemon grass. Leave it for two minutes and throw it away. If you keep it longer, the gravy will taste bitter. This will give a sort of South eastern nations curry flavour into your meal.

(b) Take a kadai, put the chicken/mutton gravy into it. Put the heat on. In a separate pan heat some oil, put some mustard seeds, curry leaves and quite a handful of red chillies. When they start to splutter, add them into the gravy. Add half a cup of freshly prepared coconut milk. This will give a sort of Indian coastal cuisine taste to your meal.

10
Cleaning of Electronic Items

1. **DVD Players** – Use microfiber cloth or electrostatic duster at least weekly, to keep your model running smoothly. The insides of our DVD player can get dusty too. A great tool is a DVD disc cleaner. This cleaner looks just like a disc with some extra little brushes on its surface.
2. **Computer Screen** – A quick dusting with a clean soft dry cloth will do or if your screen is especially dirty, try either a commercial cleaner made for your screen type or an ammonia free glass cleaner. **Other components of a computer** –Pay special attention to the fan vents, and make sure that they aren't blocked by dust. Compressed air (vacuum cleaner) can also be a useful tool. Do not forget to dust underneath your computer and the cords to your computer which can collect dust.
3. **LCD / Plasma TV** – Use only a microfibre or 100 per cent cotton cloth. Try dry dusting first, but if needed, use water dampened cloth. You can also add vinegar to water to use as a cleaning solution. Dry quickly with a separate soft cloth. Make sure the surface is completely dry before turn.ng the television on. Do not push the screen of the television, it can cause damage.
4. **Conventional TV** – It can be cleaned with glass cleaner and a dampened soft cloth.
5. **Projection TV** – Projection televisions that have a special plastic screen over the actual television screen can be cleaned

with a damp soft cloth. The screens can be damaged by paper towels and heavy duty cleaners.

6. **Cell Phones** will only need a quick wipe down with a dry cloth or with a baby wipe during the week. If a spill happens, turn off your phone, take out the battery, and use a soft cloth with a little aftershave lotion. For sticky spills that stick in crevices, turn off your phone, and try a cotton swab dipped in the same.

How to Clean Marble

Marble is porous. Hence it absorbs liquid and is extremely sensitive to stains. Never allow a spill to set on marble, as it will stain the surface and would require deep cleaning to remove the stains. To prevent stains from ruining marble surfaces, you can add a light coat of wax, unless your marble surface is white. You can wash marble using warm water, soft bristle brush and a gentle dish washing detergent and then dry with a clean cloth. You should never use abrasive cleaners containing acids, such as ammonia or vinegar on marble surfaces as they are bound to leave scratches and fine lines.

Deep Cleaning

1. **Hydrogen Peroxide**: Follow the normal procedure;
2. **Baking Soda**: and water should be combined to make a paste to clean acid stains caused by fruit juices and vinegar.

How to Clean Suede

1. **Brush regularly with a** soft brush on your favourite suede garment or use special suede shoe brush for your shoes to prevent dirt accumulation.
2. **Dry Stains** – Use a clean dry cloth to rub. Then brush it off with a soft bristle brush. Another good option is to use the pencil eraser.
3. **Wet Stains** – Use a dry cloth/paper towel/crumbled newspaper to blot it up as quickly as possible. Allow the

suede to air dry at room temperature. Never apply artificial heat (blow dryer) because this may darken the suede and leave spots.

4. **Further Tips** – It is advisable to store coloured suede clothing in a dark closet because there are high chances of getting faded due to exposure to sunlight. Also try to cover it with a dust cloth. Stained or faded suede can be dyed to a new or darker colour.

How to Clean Copper

Moderate tarnish can be removed by applying commercial copper polish (Pitambari). You can also add a little salt to a bowl of vinegar or lemon juice and mix to make a paste. Apply the paste on the tarnish and rub gently. Wipe it dry. Dab little bit of olive oil for a bright finish. Never use steel wool to remove dirt, grime or tarnish.

Preserving Copper – Never use them in keeping acidic foods such as tomatoes, vinegar-based products, lemon juice and other fruit juices which can result in formation of toxic compound. It is advisable to use copper utensils and cookware which have a porcelain enamel finish. The coating conducts heat well, while protecting the copper and your health.

Leather Cleaning Tips

If a leather product clearly states that it should be cleaned by a professional, then follow as per the instruction and resist the temptation to experiment with your own leather cleaning concoctions. However, if your leather goods don't explicitly state that they should be professionally cleaned, then you might consider using a homemade cleaner.

Leather Clothing – To clean and freshen up smelly leather, spray the leather garment with a liquid mixture one (white vinegar and olive oil) and wipe clean with a soft cloth.

Bags and Purses – Spray a mixture containing equal parts of rubbing alcohol and water directly on the stain and wipe clean with a soft cloth.

Shoes and Belts – Apply mixture one on them. Wait for a while before wiping it dry. To get rid of hard stubborn stains, you should follow the procedure mentioned above.

Note: You can apply a thin layer of Vaseline to protect any leather products from rain and moisture.

Other things which can be used for cleaning purpose: Apply it directly to the stain and allow it to sit for a few hours before wiping off with a clean, damp cloth.

1. **Toothpaste**: (Not gel)
2. **Nail polish remover**: To erase ink stains.
3. **Hairspray**: Spray quite a number of times in a row directly on the stain.
4. **Mayonnaise**: To erase water marks from hard leather goods.

11

Advantages of Homemade Cleaner

The chemicals used in the commercial cleaner are harsh and often dangerous for children and ultimately pollute the water system. Homemade cleaners, on the other hand, are made from natural ingredients. Following are the types:

Ammonia is a substance that is produced naturally in the environment. It is found in air, water, plants, animals and soil. It does not last long in the environment because it is absorbed as a nutrient by plants, bacteria and animals, thereby not building up toxins. Therefore it is safe to use. Never combine chlorine bleach and ammonia, vinegar, or any other acid because the resultant fumes can be deadly.

Vinegar – It removes oil and grease from glass and other surfaces. It also keeps windows from fogging up. Add one cup of vinegar to four cups of water and use it directly.

Rubbing Alcohol – It evaporates quickly without streaking and can be used straight from the bottle or added to other substances.

Effective Window Cleaning Solution

- One cup alcohol, one cup water, one tablespoon ammonia and one teaspoon liquid organic dish soap.
- A few tablespoons of ammonia or white vinegar added to a bucket of warm water. This is effective even in removing paint stains and sticky spots from windows and other glass.
- You can use moistened old newspapers to clean windows.
- Clearly mark the spray bottles containing your homemade window cleaner.

- Don't clean windows when the sun is shining directly on them, as the heat quickly dries the window leaving behind some unpleasant water marks.

12

Tips for New Mothers

- Use two square pieces of sun mica to clean (throw up or baby's potty). Scramble a whole newspaper and run over the area of vomit or baby's potty, it will soak the waste, throw it in the bin. Then sprinkle some phenyl and dettol over the affected area. Then wipe that area with a damp cloth. Wash the sun mica pieces with water from the commode shower.
- If your mattress has got spoilt from baby's urine, wash that area with a damp hand towel and liquid hand wash. Wipe it off with another one soaked in Dettol/Savlon/Old Spice. Then let the mattress dry with the help of blower or a fan.
- If your mattress has got spoilt from baby's vomit, use a newspaper to absorb the waste. Then repeat the same procedure as above.

Experts Tip of how to Feed Vegetables and other Nutricious Ingredients to your Children who are Fussy Food Eaters

1. Make pancakes with eggs, maida, salt/sugar and milk **OR** maida, yogurt, water and salt/sugar.
3. Make salty stuffing with sautéed vegetables of your choice.
4. Make sweet stuffing with dry fruits / honey/condensed milk/ leftover sweets.
5. Make vegetable chapati/paratha/puri with stuffing as puree of spinach/grated carrot and beet/cabbage/cauliflower/ mashed potato/mashed green peas/boiled sweet corn. Just temper the stuffing with cumin seeds and chopped onions and sauté with a bit of Indian seasoning (coriander powder, chilli powder/turmeric/roasted masala powder/finely grated

coriander leaves). You can also add grated cheese to make it more **Cheesy**.

Note: While making gobi / muli paratha, after grating, mix it with salt and keep it for half an hour. After that squeeze the stuff and drain the water. Then proceed as usual.

5. Make sweet chapati/paratha/puri with stuffing as grated pumpkin and jaggery mix/coconut and jaggery mix/sesame seeds, crushed roasted peanuts and jaggery mix. Just cook the stuffing in a heavy bottom vessel till it reaches a semi dry consistency. Allow it to cool and use it as required.
6. Make pakoras with gram flour/maida and finely chopped vegetables. Try giving it as a snack. You can add boiled, mashed potatoes and give them a desired shape. Shallow fry it and you can serve as filler for sandwiches/burgers with added spreading of butter/mayonnaise/ketchup and lettuce/ cucumber/tomatoes/onion rings, etc. You can also make kofta curry if you have adolescents at home.
7. You can make vegetable balls with flour, chopped garlic and dash of pepper. Try making vegetable manchurian/ Schezwein / chilli/sweet and sour with them.
8. While soaking rice or dal for dosa or idli, try adding a teaspoon of methi seeds. Believe me, it will not affect the taste but make it more crispy and nutritious.
9. While making kheer you can add a spoonful of methi, jaggery and coconut milk instead of cow milk.

13
An Organised Home

Here are the four most important areas to organise:

1. Organising the kitchen and other kitchen related items.
2. Arrange the cabinet or cupboard in the kitchen to store kitchen appliances and gadgets. Many items are bought out of impulse, and often we aren't even aware of how much we have accumulated over the years.
3. Use trays and boxes to hold similar items together, so that they are easier to locate, retrieve and put back.
4. There are a host of contemporary storage solutions the modern age has to offer-right from modular kitchen to custom made regular cabinets. Depending upon your affordability, go and get whatever suits you the best to organise your kitchen.
5. **Another option, in case you cannot afford 'a done up kitchen' is–you can get a bright colourful curtain matching with the colour of the kitchen tiles to cover those areas (concrete/wooden/metal shelves) where you are stocking all your kitchen essentials. This way you can also hide away the unsightly essential items.**
6. Keep your products which otherwise appears bulky in product packaging in plastic containers of varying sizes to occupy less space.

One common problem faced by most homemakers is wasting time in trying to find the right lid for the right container. By following a few simple steps you will save a lot of time.

1. Toss or recycle any containers whose lids are missing, or lids whose containers are missing. This will save you a lot of time trying to locate them.
2. Keep containers piled together by shape: rounds together, rectangle together and square together. Best way is to store them in the descending pattern.
3. Keep similar shaped lids in the same zip lock bags. Use two-three zip lock bags, depending on the amount of lids that you have.
4. Keep bags in upright position to avoid spillage.
5. Always develop the habit of putting containers and lids back in the same place from where you have found them.

Store kitchen Appliances by Use

Three Rules of Thumb:

1. Frequently used appliances go on your counter top, or the lowest shelves in your cabinet.
2. Rarely used appliances are stored at the top of your kitchen cabinet.
3. Never used items need to be re-assessed and donated or sold.

Suggestions

1. Try to cut down the amount of appliances you keep handy. Furthermore, try to limit the appliances, which have similar use. e.g.; A blender can be used for fruit juice, blend smoothies, thin soups and act as a basic food processor, while a rice cooker is really just a one-trick master. Always be realistic, unless you are really making up batch of homemade Momos/modaks (steamed dumplings) each weekend, do you really need a Momo maker taking up valuable cabinet space? It's important to own appliances that perform multiple uses. **Examples:** A food processor promises you to give a series of benefits in the long run. A tumbler or a pressure cooker can

produce perfectly cooked rice. There is really no need for a rice cooker unless you use it daily.

2. Wrap the cord around an appliance before storing in your cabinet.
3. Buy a **Step-stool** to store appliances on higher shelves.
4. Store smaller-parts (think of all those food processor attachments, icing cones, jalebi maker, kulfi moulds) in zip lock bags and label them.
5. Give it a good cleaning: first dust, then wipe cabinets with a damp cloth followed by a dry cloth.
6. Try to go through your cabinets at least once a month.
7. Label each shelf ('dishes', 'wine glasses', 'food processor', etc.).
8. Keep an inventory list taped to the cabinet door or write every detail in the housekeeping diary.

Kitchen Storage Solutions

You can free up counter space for chopping and kneading with the kitchen storage solutions available in the market. Else ask a good carpenter to design it as per your specifications (you can get ideas from a furniture catalogue). Whether you have a large kitchen with abundant storage space, or a small kitchen with limited space, there is always a need to invest in cabinets and covers to optimise the free space in the kitchen.

Junk Drawer

This type of drawer is usually necessary in a kitchen to hold twisters, rubber bands, scissors, match box for candles, pens and paper, just to name a few. I advise you to thoroughly go through these items and segregate all those items that do not belong to the kitchen or are not in use. If they are in working condition, you can donate them or give them away to friends or family members. The idea is to eliminate the junk and keep only the things you use! An easy and affordable way to manage the drawer is to invest in a drawer organiser. If it is not affordable to you, then use several plastic boxes, cut some rectangular strips from piece boards and place them inside the drawer to make several compartments.

Food Storage Containers: They should be clear and transparent to be eligible for storing left over in the refrigerator.

Wall Mounted Spice Rack: can accommodate all the bottles of spices you need.

Bake Ware and Tray Holders: These items can be a challenge to organise because they take up a lot of space, they can be hard to reach, and usually when you remove one piece, the rest of them fall over like dominoes. Either conceal it on your countertops, or you can try storing it in your lower cabinets, to free up counter space.

Pots and Pan Storage: A great way to keep your pots and pans within reach and to maximize your space is to consider a pot rack or to store them in your lower cabinets.

Under Sink Storage: If it is considerably big, you can store detergents, liquid soap dispensers, soap bottles and kitchen cleaning supplies apart from your dustbin.

Wrap storage: Cling film/plastic wrap, butter paper, aluminum foil and storage bags should be stored at an eye level storage place for easy access.

Plastic Grocery Bags: Small size grocery bags need not be stored and big ones can be neatly folded and stored in a bigger bag.

14
Organising A Freezer

It allows one to cook and store in bulk and prepare readymade meals ahead of time.

1. In order to determine what needs to be thrown out and what needs to be kept, first remove everything from the freezer.
2. Clean your freezer first.
3. Check the expiry date to decide. For repackaged items (leftovers, non-veg items) check their freezer expiration dates (FED).
4. Repackage existing items (both leftovers and new items). For example, if you have a half empty box of candies or Bengali sweets, transfer them to a zip lock bag. Don't forget to write FED.
5. Plan your meal in advance. Example you bought two kg chicken, two varieties of fish and half kg prawn. Storing them by repackaging in cooking serving sizes would optimise the storage space.
6. Try to pile items on top of each other or beside each other. Meats and chicken together (not in the same packaging of course) and frozen vegetables on another shelf.

15
Organising Your Recipes Collected From Various Sources

Recipes can come from several different sources e.g., cookbooks, websites, cookery shows, newspaper clippings, magazines, family and friends. You can consider some of the tips given below on how to store and organise your favourite recipes.

Expandable File Folder

These file folders can be purchased in almost any store that sells stationeries, school items and other office supplies. They are affordable and available in many colours and styles. The number of pockets you will require will depend on the amount of categories you wish to use.

Steps

1. Label each pocket according to the name of the categories e.g. Appetizers, Breakfast, Snacks, Cocktails, Mocktails, Lunch, Dinner, Accompaniments, Dessert, etc.
2. Now you can subdivide each category into two or more sub parts like Indian, Continental, Multicuisine, etc.
3. Next you can further subdivide according to your convenience.

Examples

4. Chicken, Mutton, fish and egg should fall under Non-Veg
5. Mushrooms, Vegetables Paneer should fall under Veg.
6. South Indian, Gujarati, Bengali, Parsi etc., should fall under

Indian.

7. Lebanese, Thai, Chinese should fall under continental.
8. Pizza and breads, Salads Stews and soups, Stir fry should fall under accompaniments.
9. Sweets, Ice creams, Apple pie should fall under dessert.

If you are able to arrange your recipes in the aforesaid manner, it will not only help you save time in searching for them, it will also prevent cluttering. You can pass down these precious recipes from one generation to another.

16

Kitchen Storage Ideas

Tupperware or Lock and Lock containers are easy to use and great for storing food in the refrigerator. One other option is airtight glass storage containers.

Some More Storage Ideas

Before shelling out extra money, always remember one thing. Scan the area available through your eyes. Whether you can utilise the existing storage available in the cabinets, walls or any corners of the room? If yes, go ahead, unleash your ideas and give them a realistic application with the help of the following ideas. I bet, you will be thrilled to see the amount of extra storage you get without investing in additional shelves and so on.

1. **Wall Hooks** – Even if you don't have the room for a hall tree, you definitely need these wall hooks to hang jackets, everyday used items, etc.
2. **Over the Door Storage Rack** – Ideal to store books, CDs and DVDs while allowing you to utilise an existing space that we don't normally consider using. Example – The wall area on top of the door, back of the door, etc.
3. **Expanding Coat Rack** – If you are a proud owner of pet and your daily schedule comprises of walking the dog, this idea is definitely meant for you. This is ideal to hang up jackets, umbrellas, accessories for the pet like collars, leashes, etc.
4. **Stacking Cubes**- If you have enough wall space, you can install these cubes to store a host of different items which

are very essential for day-to-day purpose such as brief cases, incoming as well as outgoing laundry, children's school supplies and accessories, etc. These are functional as well as economical.

Note: The outgoing laundry could be neatly placed inside a big shopper bag while the incoming should be further accompanied with a plastic bag, big enough to hold the pressed clothes in shape. Idea is to hide away the unsightly messy clothes to be laundered.

5. **Cleaning/Laundry Kit** – You don't need to buy this unnecessarily. Take any old big mug, small bucket where you can stock all your cleaning essentials like scrubber, washing soap, a bottle of hydrogen peroxide, a bottle of phenyl, a broom, a mop, etc.
6. **Key Holder** – There are a variety of attractive affordable holders available in the market that will help you organise all your keys in one place.

   Note: Never hang your personal/valuable closet's key on this key holder.

17

Daily Clean Up of The Kitchen

1. Keep things clean and dry. Don't procrastinate. Whoever handles the kitchen should be trained to use the wet and dry towel. The wet towel is meant for cleaning all the bottles after you are done up with the day's cooking. The dry towel is meant for your hands whenever you feel the need to wipe them.
2. These clothes can be washed once in two or three days along with other kitchen and dusting clothes.
3. Fill a large tumbler with hot boiling water. Put some washing powder into it and half lemon. Now put all the soiled clothes into it and put it on low flame. When it starts to boil, put it off and allow it to soak overnight. Next morning you will be amazed to find them so clean and fresh after a regular wash.
4. Nowadays, every kitchen boasts of several gadgets. To keep them in good condition you should always take good care of them. Never leave them unclean. First get away with the dry dust as is common from the toaster, griller, microwave, etc., then clean them with a sponge and a little of homemade solution. In case you don't have time, the exterior can be wiped off with Collins.
5. Now to prevent them from regular dirt and grime in the kitchen always cover it up. If you don't get a cover for your appliances, then buy some fancy small clothes and cover it up. Give them an attractive look by fixing a cloth clip at the back of the cover.

Tip – You can use an old pillow/cushion cover to cover a mixie/food processor. (Cut along the length of it and stich along the width.)

6. Whenever you are doing up large quantity of fish or any other non-veg. item, always boil a piece of lime in a tumbler of water with the kitchen clothes. It will serve two purposes. Your clothes will get clean and your kitchen won't smell like a fish market.
7. Clean up spills as and when they occur to avoid other things getting messy. It is very pleasant, refreshing and inspiring to enter a clean kitchen with a clean and empty sink in the morning.
8. Prefer using paper towels and washable sponges for cleaning the countertops. Former can be discarded whereas the later can be washed and disinfected in warm soapy water.

Weekly Clean Up for the Kitchen

1. To clean thick grease build-up on the kitchen cabinets, you can use baking soda and plenty of hot water.
2. Once in a week, religiously follow this regime-switch off the refrigerator remove all the food. Clean all the shelves, trays, vegetable basket, chiller trays, inside and outside the refrigerator with warm soapy water. Place a small container with baking soda. If possible try to have a make shift arrangement for the day's meal or you can arrange to get it from outside. You can sort out what leftovers you have. You can mix all non-veg items and make one dish and all veg items together will make another dish.

   Tip – Saute some Onions, put washed and drained rice. Add seasonings. Put two whistles. Then add all the leftovers, mix well, cover and cook for a few more minutes. Serve this delicious khichri with accompaniment of your choice. After you are through with the cleaning, place all the food items back again.

3. Wash dustbins once a week and also clean the area surrounding it.
4. Use an insect repellent once a week, around the dustbin area especially, at night before going to bed. It should be ensured all food items are properly kept.
5. While chopping fruits and vegetables, always do it on top of a newspaper, so that you can throw away the scraps and remains containing the mess at one go either in the dustbin or straightaway to your kitchen garden as vermi-compost manure.
6. Identify the corners of the kitchen which normally gets cluttered. Try to clear those spots and follow a strict discipline in keeping things in the correct place. Also ensure members/ maids who handle the kitchen to follow this schedule.

Yearly Maintainance of the Kitchen

Try to apply a single coat of polish to your clean kitchen cabinets if possible. This will help prevent build up of termite deposits.

1. Take help from professional pest control people. You can try a commercial product on weekly basis.
2. If your kitchen comprises of tiles, get it scrupulously cleaned by professional help.
3. If your kitchen wall does not comprise of tiles, get it painted once in every year.

18

Making Up of A Bathroom

Store Cleaning Supplies in the Bathroom

You can save a lot of time in cleaning your bathroom by creating an exclusive bathroom cleaning kit that you can safely store in the bathroom. It should consist of a daily shower spray, a scrubber, a hard toothbrush, a squeezee/table mop/a wash cloth.

Note: Refer to my Toothbrush as a cleaning tool

Cleaning Shower Heads

Sometimes we find that the holes of the shower head get clogged, which eventually results in less water pressure. This is mainly due to the lime and mineral deposits present in hard water. You can warm some vinegar in a microwave and pour into a zip lock bag large enough to cover your shower head. Leave the shower head in the warm vinegar for about an hour. After that, you can use a toothbrush to clean off any remaining mineral deposits. Rinse in warm water.

Care of the Walls

Always keep a cloth or squeezee in your shower to wipe down the walls as soon as you have finished bathing. It's best to tackle the problem while the shower walls and doors are still wet.

Apply a paste of baking soda and hydrogen peroxide to the grout in your bathroom tiles. Rub them with an old toothbrush and let it sit for an hour. Rinse by cleaning with a damp sponge. For heavy and stubborn stain, you can use some bleach. The two aforesaid cleaners are also effective in neutralising the smell of urine that sometimes occur in toilets used by many people.

Sprinkle some Borax onto the affected area to remove hard water stains. Let it sit for a few minutes and wipe with a damp sponge.

Cleaning of a Bathtub

Even with regular cleaning, a bathtub is bound to turn yellow. This is mainly due to the mineral deposits. Apply a paste made from cream of tarter and peroxide to remove unsightly yellow stains from the bathtub. Scrub the tub with a brush and rinse thoroughly.

To Clean Chrome Fixtures

Apply a paste of baking soda and dish washing liquid to the fixtures and rub clean with a cloth.

To Clean Brass Fixtures

Apply a paste made up of equal amount of baking soda and lemon juice. Clean in the same way.

To Prevent Mold and Mildew in the Bath Mat

Always remember to hang it after each use and try to keep it dry as far as possible. You can wash it in the washing machine or use Borax to clean and disinfect.

Defogging the Bathroom Mirror

You can try rubbing the mirror with shaving cream and clean it well with a soft cloth afterwards. If you don't have enough time in your hand, target the blow dryer towards it and it will get clear in a jiffy.

Bath Towels

After a bath or shower, water softens the top layer of our skin. Bath towels that we rub all over our bodies pick up these microscopic bits of skin and get trapped in the fibres. Eventually, after enough use, the fibres become overloaded with skin cells and give off a repelling odour. The same thing also happens with kitchen and dusting cloths. You can pre-treat them with bleach if they are White. You can also try something which I normally do. After soaking your white garments in bleach overnight, don't throw away the bleach water. Instead use it to soak all your clothes which are in dire need of freshness. Soak them for one hour and then wash in the usual way. I have found that the fading property of the bleach vanishes after a couple of hours but the prominent smell of the bleach cum disinfectant still remains. Thereby your non white colours will not fade, they will be cleansed and will smell fresh as well.

To clean the nooks and corners – Refer to my Toothbrush as a cleaning tool.

To remove mineral deposits on the bathroom faucet

Moisten a few paper towels in white vinegar and wrap them around the faucet like a cocoon. In the morning, remove the towels. Refer to my Toothbrush as a cleaning tool.

Pre-treatment

Spray the cleaning liquid upon the shower, sink and toilet and let it sit for a while. You can utilise this time to pick up clutter, clean out the medicine / toiletries cabinet, clean the refrigerator or do some makeover with your furnishing accessories.

Using a daily Shower Spray

You can use a daily shower spray/a cleaning liquid to use it after you are done in the shower. Spray down the walls, doors, and/ or curtain. Many shower sprays will help prevent buildup and keep your shower looking fantastic.

Squeegee or Wipe Dry

Give your shower a quick wipe down with a squeegee or a towel to prevent buildup.

How to Clean Shower Curtains

Pre-spray the curtain with your shower cleaner and throw it in the washing machine and wash normally. Take out the shower curtain out of the washing machine when the cycle is over and hang it up again in the bathroom. Never rinse.

Scrub Down the Toilet.

To keep the bathroom floor dirt free:

1. One of the best ways to get a floor effectively clean is to use a scrubber and detergent and use your right toe to scrub the floor. Finally wipe it off by scooting the floor mop around the floor with your feet. It provides more contact and pressure to effectively clean the floor. Be extremely careful and slow to avoid accident.
2. Empty and wash out the trash can. Put a liner to keep it clean.
3. Use a dry paper towel to wipe up the remaining hair and dirt that is left on the toilet floor.

Sliding Shower Door

This type of door is made up of four tracks that the doors slide on (two on top and two on bottom), and then the doors themselves. Generally people don't have difficulty in keeping the doors clean; it is the bottom tracks that cause the problems. Soapy water runs into the tracks from the door and pools there. People don't normally think about drying the tracks out after a shower so the puddle of water can sit in the track eventually causing slippery soap scum or even. As dirt collects in the bottom track, it can cause the tracks to become damaged, causing difficulty in sliding the door.

Sliding shower doors should be cleaned first from the inside and then outside.

Note: Keep in mind that sliding shower doors often need to be replaced after 12 to 15 years of use.

Steps for Cleaning

1. Wear old clothes before you start your cleaning spree.
2. Spray the cleaning liquid (undiluted white vinegar or bleach)

from a spray bottle upon any mould or mildew. Allow to stand while you work.

3. Get inside the shower.
4. Dip the squeegee/a rag in water and scrub the inside of the doors with it until all the soap scum is gone. Rinse the doors with clear water and removes the excess water with the squeegee.
5. Step out of the shower and repeat the process on the outside.
6. To remove stubborn mineral buildup on glass shower doors, apply a paste made up of equal amounts of baking soda and salt. Clean as usual.
7. Spray some bathroom cleaner on a paper towel and wrap the towel around the bristle end of the toothbrush. Then scoot the brush along the tracks to dislodge dirt. Rinse with clean water and dab with a dry rag.

Maintaining the Shower Doors Clean

- Wipe out the tracks after your shower.
- Clean it on a weekly basis is a good idea.
- Running a bar of paraffin wax over the track when it is clean will help it resist dirt and damage.
- Use a squeegee to get the water off the doors after each shower.

19

Overall Cleaning of the House

1. Dust Down the Ceiling and Corners
2. Never spray cleaner or water onto any picture frame. The liquid can seep behind the glass and damage the pictures. Instead use a damp cloth to wipe the frame and glass.
3. Dust the Vents and Fans.
4. Take down light fixtures and gently wash and dry them before replacing.
5. Take down draperies, curtains, blinds, etc. to wash or get it cleaned according to the directions
6. Dust down any blinds and wash windowsills and corners. Wash the inside and outsides of windows. Take down and rinse off screens, before replacing.

20

Organising Your Furnishing Closet

1. **You can try going for monochromatic colour.** Nothing will make your linen closet look more organised than monochromatic sheets, towels, pillow cases and covers. Don't ever think they might become too boring. You can create fun by splashing colours all around. Make the most of it by colourful rugs, durries and throwaway cushions.
2. **Label the shelves.** It becomes easier and quicker for each member of the family to get whatever they want. You should also label the baskets or topless bins where you have neatly folded your furnishings.
3. **Iron all the contents.** A closet looks better if all its contents are ironed and neatly kept. Sheets will fold more easily and your bed will look cozy and inviting.

21

How to Care for the Mattress

1. To provide even wear, flip the mattress every six months, so that the top is now on the bottom, and turn it so that the foot of the mattress is now at the head.
2. You can use a mattress cover to protect the mattress.
3. To remove dust from the mattress surface, vacuum the mattress using the upholstery attachment on your vacuum cleaner. To me, the Indian coconut stick broom works the best.
4. If the mattress surface becomes dirty or soiled, refer previous pages.

Making Up of a Bed

A beautifully made bed or a stack of fresh towels is not only appealing but also refreshing. It seems so easy to leave the bed in a state of jumbled mess when you wake up. Most people do not tidy it thinking that they are going to any way mess it up again in a matter of few hours. Making a bed has become one of those chores that very few people bother with, but a made bed has a dramatic impact on the way a room looks and feels. Here are a few simple steps to make a bed, and make your room appear more organised. If you have children at home, try to train them from a very small age to maintain their beds.

1. **Put the bedsheet on** – If it is fitted, simply slip the corner pockets onto the ends of the bed and adjust the fitted sheet around the mattress. If it is flat, arrange the sheet by folding in the usual way.

2. **Place the top sheet** – Place the top sheet evenly on the bed, and fold under with hospital corners only at the end of the bed.
3. **Place a Blanket During Winter** – If you don't have a proper place to keep the blanket, you can also place the blanket on top of the made bed with the top folded along the pillows.
4. **Add Pillows** - To place pillows under the blanket, fold the top sheet down over the blanket. Place pillows flat on the top sheet at the head of the bed. Fold blanket over the pillows towards the head of the bed, and smooth. Pillows can also be laid upright against the head of the bed.
5. **Throw some cushions to give that perfect finished look.**

22

Plants for your kitchen window

Tulsi – The tulsi or basil is an important symbol in the Hindu religious tradition and is worshipped in the morning and evening by Hindus. The holy basil provides herbal remedy for a lot of common ailments.

Lemon grass – This herb cherished for its aroma and citrus cum ginger taste. It is widely used in Thai, Malaysian and Vietnamese cuisine. It is also widely used in making flavoured tea, Thai food and various types of soup.

Kafir lime – Along with lemon grass and galangal, kaffir lime peel is the basic ingredient of most Thai curries, giving a complexity of flavour that distinguishes them from Indian curries.

You can also keep *Curry* Plant and *Pudina* Plant.

23

Celebrate Your Festivals with Great Cheers

Everybody wants to get together and bond with their family and friends during festivals, be it Holi, Diwali, Durga Puja, Id or Christmas. So why not think of some special décor for the house during these occasions, which will make you feel good and is inviting to your guests too.

Ideas to Give a Festive Look to your 'Home Sweet Home'

Think of setting the table. You don't have to possess an expensive piece of furniture to suit the need. Invest in a rich tablecloth in terms of colour (shades of red, green and gold) and texture. This is the most important piece of festive décor. Choose the right shade of napkins to go with the colour of the table cloth. Don't just place the napkins on the table. Be innovative and fold them in different ways or use napkin rings. Place table mats available in different sizes and colours. I prefer the cotton ones over the plastic ones because the former gives a rich and classy look. You can place an artistic table runner across your dining table to place hot serve ware. This will also stand out as a unique piece of décor. To create a magical ambience for a beautiful dinner you can opt for votive holders available in various colours and shapes. If you are having small children at home, it may not be possible to light T–lights. In that case, you can opt for LED votive holders.

Last but not the least which should be a must for every table is **Multi functional utility basket** (either in cane/metallic wire or brass) where you can place a variety of fruits in your own style. If you have small children at home or you have them in your guest list, you can also place a simple or decorative **Candy jar** with assorted candies and marsh mellows inside it. The little ones will be thrilled at the sight of it.

During festivals, holidays and vacations, people tend to visit friends and family. Pay attention in cleaning the public areas of your home where guests will be spending the majority of their time like entrance of the house, kitchen, floors and bathrooms. Keeping one's home clutter free is the greatest challenge people face when preparing for their guests arrival. Keep your counters and common living areas free from unnecessary furniture, children's toys and stacks of holiday greeting cards. If you follow my earlier suggestions related to de-cluttering, you should not face any problem at all. If there is constant coming and going of guests, simply take care of a few things:

1. See that you have a few extra towels so that you can provide one fresh for every wash basin you have at home.
2. Also ensure that the wash basins are clean and the liquid soap dispenser bottles are filled up.
3. If they are staying overnight, ensure the bed sheet and the pillow cases are clean. Also don't forget to offer them a fresh towel.
4. Take extra pain to get the toilet clean and provide a fresh new bathing soap and a washing bar for your guests.

Important Point to Remember

Cleaning need not be stressful if done in a proper and planned way. It can actually be fun and relaxing. Turn on your favourite music and enjoy while cleaning. Get your kids involved too! It's a great way to spend time together. You can start by teaching them the suggestions mentioned in this book and encourage them to follow them. You can give them incentives (remember not bribes) like going out for a movie together/dinner outside etc. if they are taking care of their toys, puzzles, art and drawing materials, hobby things, etc., the way you told them to.

24

Some Serving Ideas

1. Make a dip by mixing yogurt with tomato ketchup/mint/coriander chutney. Add seasoning and chaat masala (optional). Serve this dip with any papads, wafers, pakoras, stuffed parathas, etc. You can also serve this as an alternative for raita to go with any rice dishes.
2. Make various toppings like square or round pieces of cheese and a dollop of tomato ketchup. You can substitute cheese with boiled egg slices or shredded chicken. Try various shapes cutouts from fruits like mangoes, pineapples, musk melons, cherries, strawberries/round slices of tomato. These toppings can go very well over any crackers/salted biscuits.
3. If you are working and you do not have time, you can go for frozen foods like smiley fries, French fries, vegetable/chicken tikkies, nuggets, burger patties, salamis, sausages, etc.
4. You can also buy some cans of baked beans. Heat them, spread them over your toast and serve.
5. You can make homemade yummy smoothies with milk or yogurt blended with mangoes, apples, chickoos, bananas, cantaloupes, muskmelon, strawberries, kiwis, dates (soaked overnight in hot milk) etc. Serve chilled in tall slender glasses. You can sprinkle a handful of finely chopped dry fruits/even crushed chikkis over it. Fruit smoothies are not only tasty and healthy but are quite filling and a great alternative to having a snack.
6. You can make the following salad which is a very healthy

snack by itself. Mix some corn kernels (steamed), chopped tomatoes, onions, capsicum, juice of half a lime, a pinch of seasoning and a drizzle of olive oil. Toss it and serve. It is delicious, sweet and crunchy.

7. You can also serve an all time favourite - cocoa milk. Serve hot or cold. You can top it with a little bit of choco chips if you want to.
8. You can prepare some garnishing items in advance in case you are planning to serve drinks to your guests like lime wedges, a few sprigs of mint leaves, finely chopped coriander leaves, dry fruits, sliced cherries, a few rose / marigold petals, etc.
9. **Fondue** is perfect for any kid's party celebrations. I received a wonderful Fondue set from my baropishi, a few years back and try to put it in good use whenever possible. Normally I use it in 2 ways.

   Chocolate – I like to arrange a set of small bowls or a big platter which can hold ***fruits*** like sliced bananas, apples, pears, pineapples, orange sections, strawberries, cherries, grapes, dried fruits, etc. You can also put marshmallows or even bite size sponge cake pieces.

   Cheese – Here I use ***roasted*** vegetables like red bell pepper slices, celery sticks, potato wedges, sweet potatoes, cherry tomatoes, mushrooms, ***blanched vegetables*** like broccoli, asparagus, green beans, snow peas, etc. You can also use toasts and cubes of multi-grain breads, tortilla chips, croissants, bread sticks, wafers, etc.

25

Ideas to Make Your Small Room Look Bigger

1. You have to design concepts that create illusions of spaciousness.
2. Painting with light colours make the rooms look bigger, brighter, open and airy. Dark shades on the other hand makes it look smaller.
3. Try out colour combos. Cream/white with baby shades like baby pink, sky blue, lemon yellow, light sea green, peach and light orange.

   Note : Choosing any one or combination of two basic colours have one advantage. Soft furnishing items like table linen, bed linen, cushions, etc., can be interchangeable as most of the colours go with the basic ones.
4. Paint your wall trim and mouldings a lighter shade than your walls. This will help the wall appear further back.
5. Try to keep the floor vacant as much as possible. Don't use any durries or rugs.
6. Use furniture which has a versatile use.

Examples:

(a) A chest/old trunk with a colourful cover can serve as a coffee table.

(b) A sofa cum bed to accommodate your guests.

7. A divan with storage facilities where you can store your winter blankets, off season garments, etc.

8. Folding dining table / workstation where you can use your laptop in the night and use it to have your food in the day time.
9. Place large furniture against the walls to have more open space in the middle. Try to keep furniture of the same colour as that of the wall.
10. Place a mirror on any of the walls. It tends to increase the area of the room due to the reflection it creates.
11. Use window glass panes to allow natural light to come in as much as possible. Glass and mirrors can do wonders in transforming any cluttered, claustrophobic ambience into an open, aesthetically, pleasing surrounding. Use glass in windows, tables, mirrors, decorative shelves, corner shelves, etc., to give spacious appearance. You can use lamps of any type to make the room appear bigger and brighter.
12. Use curtains of monochromatic colour.

Optimising the Area of Your Home

1. If you have a rectangular space at the entrance of your home, you can place a chest drawer with a good oval shaped mirror on top of it. It can serve as a decorative as well as functional item. You can also keep a shoe cabinet to store family member's shoes.
2. You can use wooden, carved partition to separate a room into two sections. This can ensure privacy as well serve the very purpose of owning a separate space by itself.

Example:

(a) In the living room, dining and living area.

(b) In the bedroom, bed and workstation.

(c) In children's room, children's area and a small area meant for guest.

Homes with High Ceilings

The rules of thumb are just the opposite of what was applied for smaller homes.

1. The ceiling should be always no – white colour because it tends to make the room more spacious. Go for richer darker shades to make the ceiling look lower than it actually is.
2. You can splurge on hanging chandelier or a cluster of a few hanging lights to bring the light down to normal level. You can also light up some table lamps or bracket lights for additional lighting.
3. The best option is to hang a soft light in the centre of your dining table to create a romantic ambience.
4. You can display single photos, art, paintings only if they are enlarged or a collection of smaller pieces.
5. You can hang some long fancy wind chime in the centre of any room/near any window to catch the attention of the guests.
6. Low sitting arrangements should be definitely avoided.
7. Any sort of sleek furniture should be avoided. You can go for antique ones including long armchair or taller back chair.
8. If you possess some heirloom like metal urn, handi, use your creativity and imagination to keep them. They can be used as a centre table by fixing a glass top or can hold some fresh flowers in a pool of water. Drop some aromatic oil into the water and sail some floating candles to see the refreshing ambience you get.

26

Accessories to Complement Your Home Decor

Just like jewelry complement a woman's appearance, there are a lot of furnishing accessories that just do the same in creating the miraculous difference between two homes. Nowadays there are a lot of such readymade things available in the market.

I will give you a few real life examples.

I know one such house where the homemaker (she was my friend Sriparna's mother. I used to call her Gautami pishi) was very talented in crochet and fine embroidery. Her big table was covered with a bright colour cotton fabric bordered with a contrast colour crochet. It was plain red colour with yellow border or sometimes it was an application of appliqué motif all over with a contrast colour piping around it. Same thing went with the door curtains (bright green colour with lemon yellow border) and sometimes the sprawling bedspread on the master bedroom and the pillow covers (baby pink colour with white lacy border). The house was huge as big as a mansion. There were a couple of tall pot holders neatly placed at the entrance of every room and at each staircase landings. She used to place one of her own created crochet mats before placing the metal/earthen pots. It is three decades ago that I had seen that ambience, but still the nostalgic memories bring a feeling of joy. This made her home look unique and very special.

This example is taken from some known folks of mine who used to visit my family even before I was born. I came to know from them that there were a few old iron trunks, systematically arranged against the walls of the big hall we had. The trunks wore a thin homemade cushions made by my granny and was covered by bright colour khadi materials. In one corner of the hall one Tanpura stood upright with pride on top of one such trunk. Then there would be handmade rugs and durries made by my granny to give the room an appealing look. There was no sofa but this house with such an elegant sitting arrangement epitomized the synchronisation of aesthetics and culture personified. Courtesy my Baropishi about whom I had already mentioned.

Suggestive Ideas to Accessorise Your Home Sweet Home

1. **Living Room** – Hand woven rugs, hand knotted durries or woolen carpets. These should not be hidden under a table but should be proudly displayed to gain paeans of praise and admiration. Next comes cushions, throw it around the house to suit your taste and mood. The colours of the cover depend upon the colour of the room. If the colour of the room is too bright, then you can go for basic shades. If the colour of the room is neutral, go for bright, bold colours. If you have an artistic bent of mind, you can try doing something yourself like fabrique painting, block printing, embroidery, patchwork, appliqué work, etc. They are exotic and will also reflect your taste and persona. Another popular option available nowadays is to get the picture of your family, kids, friends, etc., embossed on the cushion cover. Last but not the least comes the floor cushions with which you can create some informal sitting arrangements.

HAPPY ENTERTAINING!

2. **Bedroom** – You can enliven your bedroom by putting up the right bedspread with matching/contrasting bedspread, etc. It can vary from cotton to satin, silk, etc., depending upon the weather and your mood. The rule of thumb for choosing

colour of the bedspread remains the same as that of cushion cover. Accessories can be a beautiful photo frame, slender shaped candle stand, a porcelain flower vase filled with fresh or good quality artificial flowers, curved shaped mirror, etc. Finish it off by a arranging a few cushions over the bed to make it look inviting and cozy.

Note: Always remember furnishings which comprise of zari borders, mirror works, sequins, art motifs or metallic colour like gold, silver and copper can be kept away for the special festive look and not for regular use.

GOOD NIGHT, SWEET DREAMS !

3. **Children's Room** – Children are very imaginative, energetic and creative. So it is important to think some themes appropriate to their age. Let us first think about their sleeping areas. You can buy readymade bunk beds; cars, cartoons, etc., shaped beds from the market or get it done by a carpenter. Their bedspread must be brightly coloured at the same time match the mental age of them. For boys you can go for Mickey mouse, Spiderman, Superman, Ben Ten, Harry Potter, etc. For girls you can go for Barbie collection, Anna Fontena, etc.

As far as their cushions are concerned, you can choose from a wide variety comprising of different shapes, sizes and colours. Try getting his/her favourite cartoon character embossed into the cushion cover to make one's belongings personalised. Another way to personalise your kid's domain is to paint one or two of your kid's favourite cartoon character on one of the walls. You can also fix some wall stickers. Last is the kid's play zone or activity area. You can throw a colourful rug/plastic mat on the floor where they can sit for hours for drawing, painting, playing with puzzles, mould some plasticin or toys. You can fix some hooks at the back of the door to hang their raincoats, umbrellas, etc. There can be a colourful toy rack which can hold toys as well as some of their story books.

Note: My personal advice is to always cover the kid's bed with a plastic colourful mat. Remove it just before their bed time. It will help you in preventing spills and dirt that normally happens in the kid's room.

HAPPY PLAYING !

Creating A Perfect Personal Space

Gone are the days when people used to enjoy their solitude in the terrace, balcony or their own room in their idle time. Now due to the space constraint, the most common problem faced by people is lack of adequate space in the house where one can relax, unwind or simply find solace just being there.

No need to worry! You can also create your own private oasis where you can read, write, listen to music, play your musical instruments, do some embroidery, meditate, do some aerobics/ yoga/dance and the list can go on. Those of you who don't want to follow any of the above said activities; even they too sometimes require a personal space to cherish their bygone nostalgic moments.

Tips for Creating Your Personal Corner

1. You should try to select that space in your house which is normally free for some time from the noise, chaos, hustles and bustles due to the regular activities.
2. It should have a good view with lots of natural light coming in. If you are not one of those lucky few, don't hesitate to invest in buying some artificial stuff to put up on the wall. This will give you a fresh feeling from within. It can be any piece of art, a pretty drape or a beautiful landscape.
3. Now place any focal object related to your field of interest.

Example

1. Avid readers may put a reading chair with a reading lamp placed near it.
2. Writers may opt for a writing desk which can also serve the purpose of holding a CD player.
3. Artists may like to put up a painting canvas stand.
4. Those of you who like to play instruments may also spread a colourful durrie or a rug to sit on it and play.
5. Try to connect yourself to nature in as many ways as possible. You can keep some indoor plants, terracotta figurines, a flower vase / an earthen pot filled with fresh flowers, an aquarium, a small fountain, a tumbler filled with sea shells / colourful pebbles / rocks.
6. Your space should reflect your own persona, your role model, your philosophy of life, etc. Try to put some favourite quotation/ picture / photo / painting through which you get tranquility, peace and inspiration. It can be a picture of your father or maybe a photo of Swami Vivekananda. It can be anything which is really inspiring to you. Meditators can keep a statue of Buddha. Aspiring dancers can keep a dancing Natraj /an idol of Jagannath. You can place a brass agarbati stand in front of it and decorate it with fresh flowers to create a magic in your daily practice.
7. If you don't have children at home, you can simply place a tray and display small curios from your personal collection. This helps in creating the right ambience.
8. To cut short, do whatever you feel like which will make you feel cozy and comfortable.
9. Try to keep your personal space free from any sort of noise in order to avoid distraction. You can hang up any wind chime if you want to or play some soft theme music like chirping of birds/gushing flow of waterfall, etc. These will really block the noise to a significant extent.

10. Pay special attention to the lighting aspect. You can go for spot lighting, coloured lighting through fancy lights, tea lights, etc. The different kind of lighting have a dramatic impact in creating the right ambience you want.
11. Last but not the least you can also try aroma therapy to satiate your soul. You may try anything from a platter of simple agarbatis, aromatic candles, essential fragrant oils, etc.
12. In a way you should try to create your personal space with all the senses you have been blessed with.

Some Common Superstitions or Myths vs Feng Shui vs Scientific/logical Reasoning

1. **Myth** – If a broken mirror is kept in the bedroom, it has a direct influence on the marital relationship between couples.

   Feng Shui – Not only a broken mirror, but anything that does not function properly is a symbol of damage and obstacles. Examples – burned out light bulb, broken lamps, torches, torn out dresses, towel, etc.

   Logical reasoning – In the home front, any such thing can hamper your happiness and mental well-being. One should get rid of such things as early as possible or try to replace them. Remember one thing, all my dear readers. This is not solely related to financial condition but cluttered state of mind which few people possess genetically. I remember my granny to use all the torn out clothes for cleaning and kitchen purpose. They were neatly trimmed and sewed and then used. After their purpose was over, she used to boil them in water with some washing soda and leave it overnight. Then in the morning, before anybody woke up, she would wash it and hang it in the clothes line to dry. She had not done any course from finishing school; neither did she possess any hotel management degree. One more thing, during that time there was no websites/magazines/books to guide her on housekeeping. Neither there were any multi coloured kitchen/ utility clothes available in the market. It was her inner most aesthetic sense which propelled her to do so.

2. **Myth** – Keep your kitchen and bathroom well lit.

 Feng Shui – This activates positive energy and prosperity in one's life.

 Logical reasoning – When there is appropriate bright light, you are inspired to work well like keeping the area around you organized and clean. On the other hand when there is dim light, it has a negative impact on the stamina and vitality of the family members. You feel dull and low.

3. **Myth** – Check, clean and dust all the art and artifacts in your home.

 Feng Shui – It is very likely that you may witness a positive change in your life.

 Logical reasoning – After following the above said advice, the ambience in your home front would drastically change to a significant extent. Then you may not fear away from the thought of socializing, mixing with friends and calling them over for tea, lunch or dinner. Chances are that through good communication and PR skills you might win someone's confidence and you are given any assignment. Success of one assignment would lead to another and so on. At the end, you would possess a sense of pride and self achievement.

BEST of LUCK!

27

Green But Brilliant Gifting Ideas

1. You can reuse wrapping papers and fix some colour pictures or logo from newspaper, magazines and calendars. Remember, it should match the thought of the recipient or the occasion.
2. You can also fix some pictures taken from cards or a mini cut out from your own drawing/painting collection.
3. Instead of fixing conventional ribbons or plastic bows, try fresh flowers or leaves or even interesting fruits like strawberries, grapes or cherries.
4. If you are using brown or white grocery bags, you can first make interesting attractive hand paintings with crayons or fabric colours and then wrap your present. You can also try some handwritten poem or slogan from newspaper, magazines and calendars. Don't forget to tie it with a unique handloom rope.
5. You can make stenciled decorative paintings done with potato or ladies finger/leaves of different shapes dipped in paint.
6. You can also give your gift wrapped in another gift.

Examples :

(a) Some accessories like earrings, bracelets can be wrapped in a scarf or a jewellery box itself.

(b) Homemade jam/jelly/pickles/papads, etc. in an attractive container.

(c) A few baby products wrapped in a baby towel in an interesting manner.

(d) Beauty products like lotion, etc. can be wrapped in a bed sheet.

(e) A cup/mug can hold pen, pencils, stationary, etc.

(f) A freshly baked cake in a cane basket tied with a napkin and a bow.

(g) Some assorted fruits/cookies in a fruit bowl or an air tight attractive container respectively.

Note: If you have kids at home, try getting idea no. 4 & 5 and five done by them.

28

Re-using Household Products to Protect Our Environment

1. Use cardboard cartons/gunny bags to store old newspaper, magazines, bottles, etc., to be sold off.
2. Use plastic bags which you get at the super stores to line the bins.
3. When renovating your house, always try to use recycled products like flooring insulation, plastic lumber, woodwork, etc.
4. Instead of buying unnecessary things from the market, try using old milk jugs, tea pots and other plastic containers to hold cleaning supplies or other essentials. With a little imagination and creativity, you can also keep plants both indoor and outdoor.
5. Perfume and drinks bottles can be used as vases or as display items.
6. If you are an artist, you can use newspaper and magazine cover as wrapping papers by giving them a few strokes of your paintbrush.
7. Leftover cement, gravel and sand can be creatively used in the garden, thereby reducing the materials going for landfill.

29

Fire Safety At Home

Source – Fire and Security Association of India.

1. Don't run electrical wires under the carpet or rug.
2. Do not overload electrical outlets.
3. Always keep a fire extinguisher at home.
4. Ensure that the gas cylinders and knobs are turned off before you leave the house, either for a few hours or for a vacation.
5. Same thing with all the electrical fittings including lights.
6. Ensure that all the electrical fittings and wires are checked and tested periodically for defects.
7. Ensure that the burning candles are placed in a safe place and they are out of children's reach.
8. If grease catches fire, slide a lid over the pan and smother the flames, then put off the burner.
9. Ensure that the cooking area is clear of combustibles like any sort of aerosol cans.
10. It is advisable to wear cotton short or tight fitting sleeves while cooking. Synthetic saree or dupatta is strictly prohibited.

30

Systematic Waste Management

1. Garbage disposal can be a pressing problem if not taken care of. There is a dire need to segregate household wastes into wet and dry waste, dispose them separately in different bags.
2. Wet waste consists of vegetable and fruits peel, food leftovers, etc. For non-veg eater, even scales of fish and egg shells do wonders as manures for plants like rose. They should be treated for vermi-composting before being used as manure for your plants.
3. Dry waste consists of any discarded plastic, metal, glass, paper, etc. which can be recycled. This group can be given to the kabadiwala directly once in a fortnight/month depending on the accumulation.

   Note: If you are one of those who can let go that extra penny earned from this, you can assign this job to your maid or driver to do it and keep the money. You will be relaxed to see it well done.
4. There is another dangerous group which consists of toxic wastes like expired medicines, batteries, dried paints, old bulbs, broken glass pieces, etc. They should be disposed of seperately.
5. Those of you, who own car, please see that neither you nor your family member should throw empty wrappers of wafers, chocolates, fruit peels, empty cans of aerated drinks, soft drink bottles and cartons, etc., on the road. I would also expect my

readers who don't own one, to follow my advice when they hire cars in their tours, travels or vacations. You can take one big plastic/grocery bag for this purpose. Keep collecting and dispose them at the point of destination, i.e. your home or hotel, etc.

Note: We don't have the RIGHT to blame others for environmental pollution and degradation, when we don't follow it ourselves.

If followed properly, it will go a long way in keeping your family members healthy, contribute to the environment as well as provide an aesthetic look to your home and society at large.

31
Do You Want to Try New Recipes?

1. Always remember to check whether you have all the necessary ingredients. Don't ever try something new when guests are coming or when you do not have adequate time.

Non – Stick Vessels and it's Cooking Spray

1. Spray the cooking barbeque grill with non-stick spray before placing the grill over the coals. Food won't stick nearly as much as it does on an untreated grill.
2. Spray your plastic storage container with nonstick cooking spray before storing tomato-based sauces or Indian curries to prevent turmeric stain.
3. Always apply a little oil (with the help of a brush) over the food to be barbequed to prevent it from sticking. Also grease the barbecue, skewers and tongs for the same reason.
4. Soaking the non stick pans in warm soapy water eases the cleaning process.
5. You can also clean the exterior of the non-stick / any other cooking vessels with Pitambari.
6. To maintain the durability, never put cold water in any hot non stick pans.

Ice – Cream

1. Store the ice cream container in a big Ziploc plastic freezer bag. This will stop ice crystals from forming when it is in the freezer.

Non – cooking Tips

1. Make a first-aid box and keep it in your kitchen, you never

know when it can come in handy. You can also make use of one of your kod's old lunch boxes. This is very essential.

2. You can sharpen a pair of kitchen scissors by cutting a sheet of sandpaper into fine strips.
3. To sharpen a sewing machine needle, stitch through a piece of sand paper.
4. To clean a blender, add a cup of warm water and a few drops of dishwashing detergent. Run it for a few seconds. Let it sit for a few seconds. Rinse clean.
5. If you are trying to move a heavy object in the kitchen such as a gas cylinder or a washing machine, pour a little washing liquid on the floor. It will slide along easily.
   Don't forget to wear rubber slippers for extra precaution.
6. Use your kitchen scissors to cut leafy vegetables into strips, shred them into small bits, chop bananas, cucumbers, carrots and other long thin fruits and vegetables into small pieces. It can be used to cut tortillas, pitas, and other flat breads into even rectangular strips. Try to keep a second pair for opening plastic packages.
7. Pre – treat tea stains from fabric with cold milk.
8. Remove chewing-gum stuck to the floor easily with the help of kerosene.
9. Remove chewing-gum stuck to clothes easily by rubbing some ice over it.
10. Remove stains from white foot wear with the help of cotton ball soaked in nail polish remover.
11. To remove candle wax from an object, hold the object close to a flame or some source of heat for a few seconds till the wax melts away.
12. To prevent silver fish from attacking your clothes, (especially zaris or zardousi work), keep a few Kalonji seeds and dried

red chilli tied in a muslin cloth in your cupboard. This really protects the clothes without discolouring the zaris.

Note : Chemicals in naphthalene balls tend to discolour the lustre.

13. To keep a vacuum flask odour free, wash it with vinegar and some hot water.
14. To remove stains from utensils, add bleaching powder in a tub of water and dip the utensils before washing with detergent.
15. While mopping the floor add two teaspoons of salt to the water to keep flies away.
16. Try cleaning ink stain from clothes with the help of cotton bud soaked in eau-de-cologne.
17. The furniture (leather) becomes shinier if it is cleaned with mixture of olive oil and vinegar/with shoe polish.
18. You can rub some wax or soap along the sides of the drawer or zippers for easy movement.
19. To increase the shelf life of the coconut halves, try putting some table salt inside it.

Different Types of Spices one must keep in her Kitchen

1. **Panch phoron** : Bengali whole spice mix (Equal proportion of cumin, black cumin, fenugreek, mustard and fennel seed)
2. Kaaalo jeere /Kalonji/onion seeds
3. **Dry roasted cumin seeds powder** : Dry roast them along with a few dry red chillies till a nice aroma comes and then grind to a fine powder.
4. **Tamarind extract** : Soak a few medium size balls of tamarind in a little warm water and take out the seeds and squeeze out the extract.
5. Hing.
6. A few Italian herbs like Oregano, Rosemary, basil, etc.

7. Assorted sauces and spread including Mustard sauce and Mayonnaise, etc.
8. Honey.
9. Cinnamon powder. [In care you want to try Apple or carrot cake] Believe me. The result is amaging.

PHOTOGRAPH

Janmashtami Celebration.

Diwali Celebration.

Magical Ambience Created by Mirror base and Arrangement of candles.

A Few Floating Diyas.

Mirror! Mirror on the Wall!.

Tea Time.

Homemade Party Cake.

Kid's Party.

Chocolate Fondue with Marshmallows and Chopped Fruits (fresh as well as dry).

Cheese Fondue with Boiled Vegetables and Crackers.

Setting the Table.

Ready for Dinner

Multi Utility Basket.

Perfect Show for the Shoe Case.

Functional Onions.

Onions Cut into 2 Halves.

The Stem End is Cut and the Remaining is Chopped and Diced as Desired Without Disturbing the Root Ends.

Onion Paste to be Fried Until Brown.

Brown Onion Paste Ready to Go Inside the Freezer.

Ginger Paste Stored in Zip Lock Bag in the Freezer.

Garlic Paste.

Ginger & Garlic Paste Kept in Zip Lock Bag and Kept in the Freezer.

3 Musketeers (Tomato Ketchup, Green Chutney & Tamarind Chutney).

Dal Bati.

Chicken Stew Food for the Soul.

Tangy Mango Chutney.

Creamy Kheer.

Author's Younger Son Who Stood First at the Science Exhibition.

Master Wardrobe.

Master Wardrobe with Section for Your Accessories.

Author with her Father.

Master Bed.

Kitchen Corner.

Stain Glass Painting on the Kitchen Wall.

Blue Potteries.

Copper, Glass and Steel Vessels.

Sparkling Non-stick Vessels and Copper Items

All Magic Done by Pitambari.

Wash Basin with Storage and Towel Holder

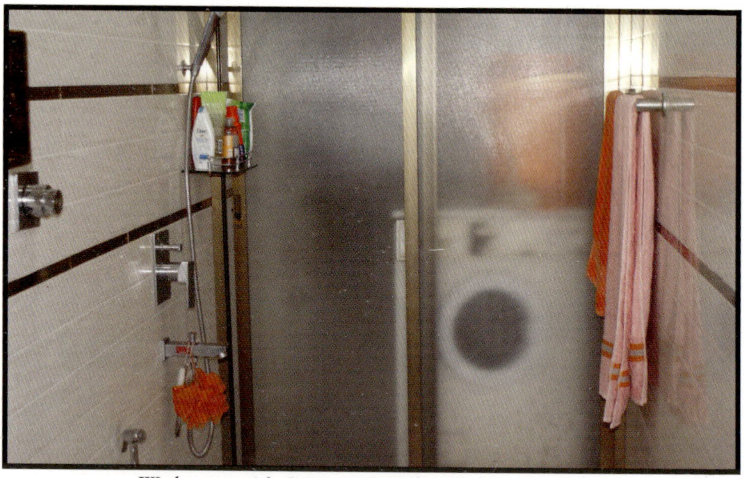

Washroom with Separate Area for Washing Machine.